T0201049

European Union Law: A Very Short Introduction

Very Short Introductions available now:

ACCOUNTING Christopher Nobes

ADOLESCENCE Peter K. Smith

ADVERTISING Winston Fletcher

AFRICAN AMERICAN RELIGION
Eddie S. Glaude Jr

AFRICAN HISTORY John Parker and
Richard Rathbone

AFRICAN RELIGIONS
Jacob K. Olupona

AGEING Nancy A. Pachana

AGNOSTICISM Robin Le Poidevin

AGRICULTURE Paul Brassley and
Richard Soffe

ALEXANDER THE GREAT
Hugh Bowden

ALGEBRA Peter M. Higgins

AMERICAN HISTORY Paul S. Boyer

AMERICAN IMMIGRATION
David A. Gerber

AMERICAN LEGAL HISTORY
G. Edward White

AMERICAN POLITICAL HISTORY
Donald Critchlow

AMERICAN POLITICAL PARTIES
AND ELECTIONS L. Sandy Maisel

AMERICAN POLITICS
Richard M. Valelly

THE AMERICAN PRESIDENCY
Charles O. Jones

THE AMERICAN REVOLUTION
Robert J. Allison

AMERICAN SLAVERY
Heather Andrea Williams

THE AMERICAN WEST Stephen Aron

AMERICAN WOMEN'S HISTORY
Susan Ware

ANAESTHESIA Aidan O'Donnell

ANARCHISM Colin Ward

ANCIENT ASSYRIA Karen Radner

ANCIENT EGYPT Ian Shaw

ANCIENT EGYPTIAN ART AND
ARCHITECTURE Christina Riggs

ANCIENT GREECE Paul Cartledge

THE ANCIENT NEAR EAST
Amanda H. Podany

ANCIENT PHILOSOPHY Julia Annas

ANCIENT WARFARE
Harry Sidebottom

ANGELS David Albert Jones

ANGLICANISM Mark Chapman

THE ANGLO-SAXON AGE John Blair

ANIMAL BEHAVIOUR
Tristram D. Wyatt

THE ANIMAL KINGDOM
Peter Holland

ANIMAL RIGHTS David DeGrazia

THE ANTARCTIC Klaus Dodds

ANTISEMITISM Steven Beller

ANXIETY Daniel Freeman and
Jason Freeman

THE APOCRYPHAL GOSPELS
Paul Foster

ARCHAEOLOGY Paul Bahn

ARCHITECTURE Andrew Ballantyne

ARISTOCRACY William Doyle

ARISTOTLE Jonathan Barnes

ART HISTORY Dana Arnold

ART THEORY Cynthia Freeland

ASIAN AMERICAN HISTORY
    Madeline Y. Hsu
ASTROBIOLOGY David C. Catling
ASTROPHYSICS James Binney
ATHEISM Julian Baggini
THE ATMOSPHERE Paul I. Palmer
AUGUSTINE Henry Chadwick
AUSTRALIA Kenneth Morgan
AUTISM Uta Frith
THE AVANT GARDE David Cottington
THE AZTECS David Carrasco
BABYLONIA Trevor Bryce
BACTERIA Sebastian G. B. Amyes
BANKING John Goddard and
    John O. S. Wilson
BARTHES Jonathan Culler
THE BEATS David Sterritt
BEAUTY Roger Scruton
BEHAVIOURAL ECONOMICS
    Michelle Baddeley
BESTSELLERS John Sutherland
THE BIBLE John Riches
BIBLICAL ARCHAEOLOGY Eric H. Cline
BIOGRAPHY Hermione Lee
BLACK HOLES Katherine Blundell
BLOOD Chris Cooper
THE BLUES Elijah Wald
THE BODY Chris Shilling
THE BOOK OF MORMON Terryl Givens
BORDERS Alexander C. Diener and
    Joshua Hagen
THE BRAIN Michael O'Shea
THE BRICS Andrew F. Cooper
THE BRITISH CONSTITUTION
    Martin Loughlin
THE BRITISH EMPIRE Ashley Jackson
BRITISH POLITICS Anthony Wright
BUDDHA Michael Carrithers
BUDDHISM Damien Keown
BUDDHIST ETHICS Damien Keown
BYZANTIUM Peter Sarris
CALVINISM Jon Balserak
CANCER Nicholas James
CAPITALISM James Fulcher
CATHOLICISM Gerald O'Collins
CAUSATION Stephen Mumford and
    Rani Lill Anjum
THE CELL Terence Allen and
    Graham Cowling
THE CELTS Barry Cunliffe

CHAOS Leonard Smith
CHEMISTRY Peter Atkins
CHILD PSYCHOLOGY Usha Goswami
CHILDREN'S LITERATURE
    Kimberley Reynolds
CHINESE LITERATURE Sabina Knight
CHOICE THEORY Michael Allingham
CHRISTIAN ART Beth Williamson
CHRISTIAN ETHICS D. Stephen Long
CHRISTIANITY Linda Woodhead
CIRCADIAN RHYTHMS
    Russell Foster and Leon Kreitzman
CITIZENSHIP Richard Bellamy
CIVIL ENGINEERING David Muir Wood
CLASSICAL LITERATURE William Allan
CLASSICAL MYTHOLOGY
    Helen Morales
CLASSICS Mary Beard and
    John Henderson
CLAUSEWITZ Michael Howard
CLIMATE Mark Maslin
CLIMATE CHANGE Mark Maslin
CLINICAL PSYCHOLOGY
    Susan Llewelyn and
    Katie Aafjes-van Doorn
COGNITIVE NEUROSCIENCE
    Richard Passingham
THE COLD WAR Robert McMahon
COLONIAL AMERICA Alan Taylor
COLONIAL LATIN AMERICAN
    LITERATURE Rolena Adorno
COMBINATORICS Robin Wilson
COMEDY Matthew Bevis
COMMUNISM Leslie Holmes
COMPLEXITY John H. Holland
THE COMPUTER Darrel Ince
COMPUTER SCIENCE
    Subrata Dasgupta
CONFUCIANISM Daniel K. Gardner
THE CONQUISTADORS
    Matthew Restall and
    Felipe Fernández-Armesto
CONSCIENCE Paul Strohm
CONSCIOUSNESS Susan Blackmore
CONTEMPORARY ART
    Julian Stallabrass
CONTEMPORARY FICTION
    Robert Eaglestone
CONTINENTAL PHILOSOPHY
    Simon Critchley

COPERNICUS Owen Gingerich
CORAL REEFS Charles Sheppard
CORPORATE SOCIAL
    RESPONSIBILITY Jeremy Moon
CORRUPTION Leslie Holmes
COSMOLOGY Peter Coles
CRIME FICTION Richard Bradford
CRIMINAL JUSTICE Julian V. Roberts
CRITICAL THEORY
    Stephen Eric Bronner
THE CRUSADES Christopher Tyerman
CRYPTOGRAPHY Fred Piper and
    Sean Murphy
CRYSTALLOGRAPHY A. M. Glazer
THE CULTURAL REVOLUTION
    Richard Curt Kraus
DADA AND SURREALISM
    David Hopkins
DANTE Peter Hainsworth and
    David Robey
DARWIN Jonathan Howard
THE DEAD SEA SCROLLS Timothy Lim
DECOLONIZATION Dane Kennedy
DEMOCRACY Bernard Crick
DEPRESSION Jan Scott and
    Mary Jane Tacchi
DERRIDA Simon Glendinning
DESCARTES Tom Sorell
DESERTS Nick Middleton
DESIGN John Heskett
DEVELOPMENTAL BIOLOGY
    Lewis Wolpert
THE DEVIL Darren Oldridge
DIASPORA Kevin Kenny
DICTIONARIES Lynda Mugglestone
DINOSAURS David Norman
DIPLOMACY Joseph M. Siracusa
DOCUMENTARY FILM
    Patricia Aufderheide
DREAMING J. Allan Hobson
DRUGS Les Iversen
DRUIDS Barry Cunliffe
EARLY MUSIC Thomas Forrest Kelly
THE EARTH Martin Redfern
EARTH SYSTEM SCIENCE Tim Lenton
ECONOMICS Partha Dasgupta
EDUCATION Gary Thomas
EGYPTIAN MYTH Geraldine Pinch
EIGHTEENTH-CENTURY BRITAIN
    Paul Langford
THE ELEMENTS Philip Ball
EMOTION Dylan Evans
EMPIRE Stephen Howe
ENGELS Terrell Carver
ENGINEERING David Blockley
ENGLISH LITERATURE Jonathan Bate
THE ENLIGHTENMENT
    John Robertson
ENTREPRENEURSHIP
    Paul Westhead and Mike Wright
ENVIRONMENTAL ECONOMICS
    Stephen Smith
ENVIRONMENTAL POLITICS
    Andrew Dobson
EPICUREANISM Catherine Wilson
EPIDEMIOLOGY Rodolfo Saracci
ETHICS Simon Blackburn
ETHNOMUSICOLOGY Timothy Rice
THE ETRUSCANS Christopher Smith
EUGENICS Philippa Levine
THE EUROPEAN UNION John Pinder
    and Simon Usherwood
EUROPEAN UNION LAW
    Anthony Arnull
EVOLUTION Brian and
    Deborah Charlesworth
EXISTENTIALISM Thomas Flynn
EXPLORATION Stewart A. Weaver
THE EYE Michael Land
FAMILY LAW Jonathan Herring
FASCISM Kevin Passmore
FASHION Rebecca Arnold
FEMINISM Margaret Walters
FILM Michael Wood
FILM MUSIC Kathryn Kalinak
THE FIRST WORLD WAR
    Michael Howard
FOLK MUSIC Mark Slobin
FOOD John Krebs
FORENSIC PSYCHOLOGY David Canter
FORENSIC SCIENCE Jim Fraser
FORESTS Jaboury Ghazoul
FOSSILS Keith Thomson
FOUCAULT Gary Gutting
THE FOUNDING FATHERS
    R. B. Bernstein
FRACTALS Kenneth Falconer
FREE SPEECH Nigel Warburton
FREE WILL Thomas Pink
FRENCH LITERATURE John D. Lyons

THE FRENCH REVOLUTION
    William Doyle
FREUD Anthony Storr
FUNDAMENTALISM Malise Ruthven
FUNGI Nicholas P. Money
THE FUTURE Jennifer M. Gidley
GALAXIES John Gribbin
GALILEO Stillman Drake
GAME THEORY Ken Binmore
GANDHI Bhikhu Parekh
GENES Jonathan Slack
GENIUS Andrew Robinson
GEOGRAPHY John Matthews and
    David Herbert
GEOPOLITICS Klaus Dodds
GERMAN LITERATURE Nicholas Boyle
GERMAN PHILOSOPHY
    Andrew Bowie
GLOBAL CATASTROPHES Bill McGuire
GLOBAL ECONOMIC HISTORY
    Robert C. Allen
GLOBALIZATION Manfred Steger
GOD John Bowker
GOETHE Ritchie Robertson
THE GOTHIC Nick Groom
GOVERNANCE Mark Bevir
GRAVITY Timothy Clifton
THE GREAT DEPRESSION AND
    THE NEW DEAL Eric Rauchway
HABERMAS James Gordon Finlayson
THE HABSBURG EMPIRE Martyn Rady
HAPPINESS Daniel M. Haybron
THE HARLEM RENAISSANCE
    Cheryl A. Wall
THE HEBREW BIBLE AS LITERATURE
    Tod Linafelt
HEGEL Peter Singer
HEIDEGGER Michael Inwood
HERMENEUTICS Jens Zimmermann
HERODOTUS Jennifer T. Roberts
HIEROGLYPHS Penelope Wilson
HINDUISM Kim Knott
HISTORY John H. Arnold
THE HISTORY OF ASTRONOMY
    Michael Hoskin
THE HISTORY OF CHEMISTRY
    William H. Brock
THE HISTORY OF LIFE Michael Benton
THE HISTORY OF MATHEMATICS
    Jacqueline Stedall

THE HISTORY OF MEDICINE
    William Bynum
THE HISTORY OF TIME
    Leofranc Holford-Strevens
HIV AND AIDS Alan Whiteside
HOBBES Richard Tuck
HOLLYWOOD Peter Decherney
HOME Michael Allen Fox
HORMONES Martin Luck
HUMAN ANATOMY Leslie Klenerman
HUMAN EVOLUTION Bernard Wood
HUMAN RIGHTS Andrew Clapham
HUMANISM Stephen Law
HUME A. J. Ayer
HUMOUR Noël Carroll
THE ICE AGE Jamie Woodward
IDEOLOGY Michael Freeden
INDIAN CINEMA
    Ashish Rajadhyaksha
INDIAN PHILOSOPHY Sue Hamilton
THE INDUSTRIAL REVOLUTION
    Robert C. Allen
INFECTIOUS DISEASE Marta L. Wayne
    and Benjamin M. Bolker
INFINITY Ian Stewart
INFORMATION Luciano Floridi
INNOVATION Mark Dodgson and
    David Gann
INTELLIGENCE Ian J. Deary
INTELLECTUAL PROPERTY
    Siva Vaidhyanathan
INTERNATIONAL LAW Vaughan Lowe
INTERNATIONAL MIGRATION
    Khalid Koser
INTERNATIONAL RELATIONS
    Paul Wilkinson
INTERNATIONAL SECURITY
    Christopher S. Browning
IRAN Ali M. Ansari
ISLAM Malise Ruthven
ISLAMIC HISTORY Adam Silverstein
ISOTOPES Rob Ellam
ITALIAN LITERATURE
    Peter Hainsworth and David Robey
JESUS Richard Bauckham
JOURNALISM Ian Hargreaves
JUDAISM Norman Solomon
JUNG Anthony Stevens
KABBALAH Joseph Dan
KAFKA Ritchie Robertson

KANT Roger Scruton
KEYNES Robert Skidelsky
KIERKEGAARD Patrick Gardiner
KNOWLEDGE Jennifer Nagel
THE KORAN Michael Cook
LANDSCAPE ARCHITECTURE
    Ian H. Thompson
LANDSCAPES AND
    GEOMORPHOLOGY
    Andrew Goudie and Heather Viles
LANGUAGES Stephen R. Anderson
LATE ANTIQUITY Gillian Clark
LAW Raymond Wacks
THE LAWS OF THERMODYNAMICS
    Peter Atkins
LEADERSHIP Keith Grint
LEARNING Mark Haselgrove
LEIBNIZ Maria Rosa Antognazza
LIBERALISM Michael Freeden
LIGHT Ian Walmsley
LINCOLN Allen C. Guelzo
LINGUISTICS Peter Matthews
LITERARY THEORY Jonathan Culler
LOCKE John Dunn
LOGIC Graham Priest
LOVE Ronald de Sousa
MACHIAVELLI Quentin Skinner
MADNESS Andrew Scull
MAGIC Owen Davies
MAGNA CARTA Nicholas Vincent
MAGNETISM Stephen Blundell
MALTHUS Donald Winch
MANAGEMENT John Hendry
MAO Delia Davin
MARINE BIOLOGY Philip V. Mladenov
THE MARQUIS DE SADE John Phillips
MARTIN LUTHER Scott H. Hendrix
MARTYRDOM Jolyon Mitchell
MARX Peter Singer
MATERIALS Christopher Hall
MATHEMATICS Timothy Gowers
THE MEANING OF LIFE
    Terry Eagleton
MEASUREMENT David Hand
MEDICAL ETHICS Tony Hope
MEDICAL LAW Charles Foster
MEDIEVAL BRITAIN
    John Gillingham and Ralph A. Griffiths
MEDIEVAL LITERATURE
    Elaine Treharne
MEDIEVAL PHILOSOPHY
    John Marenbon
MEMORY Jonathan K. Foster
METAPHYSICS Stephen Mumford
THE MEXICAN REVOLUTION
    Alan Knight
MICHAEL FARADAY Frank A. J. L. James
MICROBIOLOGY Nicholas P. Money
MICROECONOMICS Avinash Dixit
MICROSCOPY Terence Allen
THE MIDDLE AGES Miri Rubin
MILITARY JUSTICE Eugene R. Fidell
MILITARY STRATEGY
    Antulio J. Echevarria II
MINERALS David Vaughan
MODERN ART David Cottington
MODERN CHINA Rana Mitter
MODERN DRAMA
    Kirsten E. Shepherd-Barr
MODERN FRANCE
    Vanessa R. Schwartz
MODERN IRELAND Senia Pašeta
MODERN ITALY Anna Cento Bull
MODERN JAPAN
    Christopher Goto-Jones
MODERN LATIN AMERICAN
    LITERATURE
    Roberto González Echevarría
MODERN WAR Richard English
MODERNISM Christopher Butler
MOLECULAR BIOLOGY
    Aysha Divan and Janice A. Royds
MOLECULES Philip Ball
THE MONGOLS Morris Rossabi
MOONS David A. Rothery
MORMONISM Richard Lyman Bushman
MOUNTAINS Martin F. Price
MUHAMMAD Jonathan A. C. Brown
MULTICULTURALISM Ali Rattansi
MUSIC Nicholas Cook
MYTH Robert A. Segal
THE NAPOLEONIC WARS
    Mike Rapport
NATIONALISM Steven Grosby
NAVIGATION Jim Bennett
NELSON MANDELA Elleke Boehmer
NEOLIBERALISM Manfred Steger and
    Ravi Roy
NETWORKS Guido Caldarelli and
    Michele Catanzaro

THE NEW TESTAMENT
    Luke Timothy Johnson
THE NEW TESTAMENT AS
    LITERATURE Kyle Keefer
NEWTON Robert Iliffe
NIETZSCHE Michael Tanner
NINETEENTH-CENTURY BRITAIN
    Christopher Harvie and
    H. C. G. Matthew
THE NORMAN CONQUEST
    George Garnett
NORTH AMERICAN INDIANS
    Theda Perdue and Michael D. Green
NORTHERN IRELAND
    Marc Mulholland
NOTHING Frank Close
NUCLEAR PHYSICS Frank Close
NUCLEAR POWER Maxwell Irvine
NUCLEAR WEAPONS
    Joseph M. Siracusa
NUMBERS Peter M. Higgins
NUTRITION David A. Bender
OBJECTIVITY Stephen Gaukroger
THE OLD TESTAMENT
    Michael D. Coogan
THE ORCHESTRA D. Kern Holoman
ORGANIC CHEMISTRY Graham Patrick
ORGANIZATIONS Mary Jo Hatch
PAGANISM Owen Davies
THE PALESTINIAN-ISRAELI
    CONFLICT Martin Bunton
PANDEMICS Christian W. McMillen
PARTICLE PHYSICS Frank Close
PAUL E. P. Sanders
PEACE Oliver P. Richmond
PENTECOSTALISM William K. Kay
THE PERIODIC TABLE Eric R. Scerri
PHILOSOPHY Edward Craig
PHILOSOPHY IN THE ISLAMIC
    WORLD Peter Adamson
PHILOSOPHY OF LAW
    Raymond Wacks
PHILOSOPHY OF SCIENCE
    Samir Okasha
PHOTOGRAPHY Steve Edwards
PHYSICAL CHEMISTRY Peter Atkins
PILGRIMAGE Ian Reader
PLAGUE Paul Slack
PLANETS David A. Rothery
PLANTS Timothy Walker

PLATE TECTONICS Peter Molnar
PLATO Julia Annas
POLITICAL PHILOSOPHY
    David Miller
POLITICS Kenneth Minogue
POPULISM Cas Mudde and
    Cristóbal Rovira Kaltwasser
POSTCOLONIALISM Robert Young
POSTMODERNISM Christopher Butler
POSTSTRUCTURALISM
    Catherine Belsey
PREHISTORY Chris Gosden
PRESOCRATIC PHILOSOPHY
    Catherine Osborne
PRIVACY Raymond Wacks
PROBABILITY John Haigh
PROGRESSIVISM Walter Nugent
PROTESTANTISM Mark A. Noll
PSYCHIATRY Tom Burns
PSYCHOANALYSIS Daniel Pick
PSYCHOLOGY
    Gillian Butler and Freda McManus
PSYCHOTHERAPY Tom Burns and
    Eva Burns-Lundgren
PUBLIC ADMINISTRATION
    Stella Z. Theodoulou and Ravi K. Roy
PUBLIC HEALTH Virginia Berridge
PURITANISM Francis J. Bremer
THE QUAKERS Pink Dandelion
QUANTUM THEORY
    John Polkinghorne
RACISM Ali Rattansi
RADIOACTIVITY Claudio Tuniz
RASTAFARI Ennis B. Edmonds
THE REAGAN REVOLUTION Gil Troy
REALITY Jan Westerhoff
THE REFORMATION Peter Marshall
RELATIVITY Russell Stannard
RELIGION IN AMERICA Timothy Beal
THE RENAISSANCE Jerry Brotton
RENAISSANCE ART
    Geraldine A. Johnson
REVOLUTIONS Jack A. Goldstone
RHETORIC Richard Toye
RISK Baruch Fischhoff and John Kadvany
RITUAL Barry Stephenson
RIVERS Nick Middleton
ROBOTICS Alan Winfield
ROCKS Jan Zalasiewicz
ROMAN BRITAIN Peter Salway

THE ROMAN EMPIRE
  Christopher Kelly
THE ROMAN REPUBLIC
  David M. Gwynn
ROMANTICISM Michael Ferber
ROUSSEAU Robert Wokler
RUSSELL A. C. Grayling
RUSSIAN HISTORY Geoffrey Hosking
RUSSIAN LITERATURE Catriona Kelly
THE RUSSIAN REVOLUTION
  S. A. Smith
SAVANNAS Peter A. Furley
SCHIZOPHRENIA Chris Frith and
  Eve Johnstone
SCHOPENHAUER
  Christopher Janaway
SCIENCE AND RELIGION
  Thomas Dixon
SCIENCE FICTION David Seed
THE SCIENTIFIC REVOLUTION
  Lawrence M. Principe
SCOTLAND Rab Houston
SEXUALITY Véronique Mottier
SHAKESPEARE'S COMEDIES Bart van Es
SHAKESPEARE'S TRAGEDIES
  Stanley Wells
SIKHISM Eleanor Nesbitt
THE SILK ROAD James A. Millward
SLANG Jonathon Green
SLEEP Steven W. Lockley and
  Russell G. Foster
SOCIAL AND CULTURAL
  ANTHROPOLOGY
  John Monaghan and Peter Just
SOCIAL PSYCHOLOGY Richard J. Crisp
SOCIAL WORK Sally Holland and
  Jonathan Scourfield
SOCIALISM Michael Newman
SOCIOLINGUISTICS John Edwards
SOCIOLOGY Steve Bruce
SOCRATES C. C. W. Taylor
SOUND Mike Goldsmith
THE SOVIET UNION Stephen Lovell
THE SPANISH CIVIL WAR
  Helen Graham
SPANISH LITERATURE Jo Labanyi
SPINOZA Roger Scruton
SPIRITUALITY Philip Sheldrake
SPORT Mike Cronin
STARS Andrew King

STATISTICS David J. Hand
STEM CELLS Jonathan Slack
STRUCTURAL ENGINEERING
  David Blockley
STUART BRITAIN John Morrill
SUPERCONDUCTIVITY
  Stephen Blundell
SYMMETRY Ian Stewart
TAXATION Stephen Smith
TEETH Peter S. Ungar
TELESCOPES Geoff Cottrell
TERRORISM Charles Townshend
THEATRE Marvin Carlson
THEOLOGY David F. Ford
THOMAS AQUINAS Fergus Kerr
THOUGHT Tim Bayne
TIBETAN BUDDHISM
  Matthew T. Kapstein
TOCQUEVILLE Harvey C. Mansfield
TRAGEDY Adrian Poole
TRANSLATION Matthew Reynolds
THE TROJAN WAR Eric H. Cline
TRUST Katherine Hawley
THE TUDORS John Guy
TWENTIETH-CENTURY BRITAIN
  Kenneth O. Morgan
THE UNITED NATIONS
  Jussi M. Hanhimäki
THE U.S. CONGRESS Donald A. Ritchie
THE U.S. SUPREME COURT
  Linda Greenhouse
UTOPIANISM Lyman Tower Sargent
THE VIKINGS Julian Richards
VIRUSES Dorothy H. Crawford
VOLTAIRE Nicholas Cronk
WAR AND TECHNOLOGY Alex Roland
WATER John Finney
WEATHER Storm Dunlop
THE WELFARE STATE David Garland
WILLIAM SHAKESPEARE Stanley Wells
WITCHCRAFT Malcolm Gaskill
WITTGENSTEIN A. C. Grayling
WORK Stephen Fineman
WORLD MUSIC Philip Bohlman
THE WORLD TRADE
  ORGANIZATION Amrita Narlikar
WORLD WAR II Gerhard L. Weinberg
WRITING AND SCRIPT
  Andrew Robinson
ZIONISM Michael Stanislawski

Available soon:

BRANDING Robert Jones
PAIN Rob Boddice
JEWISH HISTORY David N. Myers

MULTILINGUALISM
John C. Maher
OCEANS Dorrik Stow

For more information visit our website

www.oup.com/vsi/

Anthony Arnull

EUROPEAN
UNION LAW

A Very Short Introduction

OXFORD
UNIVERSITY PRESS

Great Clarendon Street, Oxford, OX2 6DP,
United Kingdom

Oxford University Press is a department of the University of Oxford.
It furthers the University's objective of excellence in research, scholarship,
and education by publishing worldwide. Oxford is a registered trade mark of
Oxford University Press in the UK and in certain other countries

Published in the United States of America by Oxford University Press
198 Madison Avenue, New York, NY 10016, United States of America

British Library Cataloguing in Publication Data
Data available

Library of Congress Control Number: 2016958656

ISBN 978–0–19–874998–1

Printed and bound by
CPI Group (UK) Ltd, Croydon, CR0 4YY

Contents

Acknowledgements xv

Abbreviations xvii

List of illustrations xix

Introduction 1

1 What is EU law about? 3

2 From Common Market to European Union 18

3 Secondary EU law 28

4 How secondary EU law is made 47

5 On the origin of treaties 61

6 EU law in the national courts 77

7 The Court of Justice of the European Union 91

8 Enforcing EU law 99

9 Coping with crises 112

References 127

List of cases and EU measures 135

Further reading 143

Index 145

European Union Law

Acknowledgements

I benefited enormously from reading Ha-Joon Chang's *Economics: The User's Guide* (London, Pelican, 2014), which showed that it is possible to write about complex subjects in a clear and engaging way. I make no claim to having done it nearly as well as he did!

The beginning of Chapter 1 is modelled on the opening paragraphs of Richard Plender, *A Practical Introduction to European Community Law* (London, Sweet & Maxwell, 1980).

Albertina Albors-Llorens, Frances Arnull, Thomas Arnull, Alicia Hinarejos, Anne O'Sullivan, and Martin Trybus either commented on the text or discussed with me some of the issues it raises. Anonymous referees provided reassurance that the project was feasible and offered suggestions on both structure and content. I am hugely grateful to them all. In pointing out gaps, errors, and infelicities of style and forcing me to clarify my thoughts, they greatly improved the end product. Any remaining weaknesses are entirely my fault.

AA
October 2016

Abbreviations

AFSJ	Area of Freedom, Security, and Justice
CEEC	central and eastern European countries
CFSP	Common Foreign and Security Policy
CJEU	Court of Justice of the European Union
COREPER	Committee of Permanent Representatives (Comité des Représentants Permanents)
EAW	European Arrest Warrant
EC	European Community
ECB	European Central Bank
ECHR	European Convention on Human Rights
ECSC	European Coal and Steel Community
ECtHR	European Court of Human Rights
EEAS	European External Action Service
EEC	European Economic Community
EFSF	European Financial Stability Facility
EFSM	European Financial Stability Mechanism
EMU	Economic and Monetary Union
EPPO	European Public Prosecutor's Office
ESCB	European System of Central Banks
ESM	European Stability Mechanism
EU	European Union
EUI	European University Institute
HoSG	Heads of State or Government
IGC	intergovernmental conference
IMF	International Monetary Fund
MEP	Member of the European Parliament
NGO	non-governmental organization
OJ	Official Journal of the European Union

OLAF	European Anti-Fraud Office (Office Européen de Lutte Anti-Fraude)
OLP	ordinary legislative procedure
OMT	outright monetary transaction
PPU	urgent preliminary ruling procedure (*procédure préjudicielle d'urgence*)
QMV	qualified majority voting
SEA	Single European Act
SLP	special legislative procedure
SMP	Securities Markets Programme
SRM	Single Resolution Mechanism
SSM	Single Supervisory Mechanism
TEU	Treaty on European Union
TFEU	Treaty on the Functioning of the European Union
UK	United Kingdom
UKIP	United Kingdom Independence Party

List of illustrations

1   Approaching the CJEU **4**
    Court of Justice of the European Union

2   The main political institutions
    of the EU **32**

3   Appointing the Commission **41**

4   Solemn undertaking given
    by the President and members of
    the Barroso Commission before
    the CJEU (3 May 2010) **43**
    Court of Justice of the European Union

5   Campaigning in the 2016 UK
    referendum **71**
    (a) The Vote Leave Campaign
    (b) The In Campaign Limited

6   A hearing before a five-judge
    chamber of the Court of
    Justice **92**
    Court of Justice of the European
    Union

7   The members of the Court of
    Justice (February 2016) **95**
    Court of Justice of the
    European Union

8   CJEU President Vassilios
    Skouris welcomes German
    Chancellor Angela Merkel, a
    key figure in the migration
    crisis (9 March 2010) **123**
    Court of Justice of the European
    Union

The publisher and the author apologize for any errors or omission in the
above list. If contacted they will be pleased to rectify these at the earliest
opportunity.

Introduction

I once heard someone say that EU law was the only subject that law students needed to study. That remark was only partly tongue in cheek. EU law teaches us a great deal about how courts and legal systems work and about the relationship between law and economics, history, politics, and international relations. These features make EU law of interest not only to lawyers but also to anyone trying to understand one of the most ambitious attempts yet made to get historically, economically, and legally diverse nation states to work together for the common good.

If you are looking for a brief guide to the main features of EU law, this very short introduction to the subject aims to meet your needs. It will not seek to persuade you that the EU is a good or a bad thing. Its purpose is to help ensure that, whatever view you take of the EU, it is based on a proper understanding of its law and legal system. You do not have to master every technical detail to achieve that end.

Once of interest only to specialists, the EU is now the subject of great controversy. To its supporters, it has brought peace 'among peoples long divided by bloody conflicts', in the words of one of its founding documents. It has promoted democracy, human rights, and economic prosperity among its members and allowed them collectively to punch above their weight on the world stage, helping to advance European values. In 2012, the EU's contribution over six decades 'to the advancement of peace and reconciliation, democracy and human rights in Europe' led to its being awarded the Nobel Peace Prize.

Others doubt whether the political and economic advantages of EU membership are as clear as is often claimed. Their case was reinforced by the crisis in the eurozone, which led to record levels of unemployment and street protests in several countries of the EU, and the migration crisis which engulfed Europe in 2015. Others say that, even if there are economic advantages to membership, they are outweighed by the damage the EU causes to national autonomy and solidarity. Views such as these prevailed in the 2016 UK referendum on its continued membership.

Why does the EU arouse such strong passions? As an organization based on international treaties, why has it proved capable of having such far-reaching effects on its Member States and their citizens and even on countries that lie beyond its borders? Part of the explanation lies in its law and legal system, which have proved remarkably effective in ensuring that Member States respect the commitments they made when they signed those treaties. But what exactly is EU law about? And how has it become part of the legal DNA of its Member States so much more effectively than other treaty-based regimes? These are among the questions this book attempts to answer.

Chapter 1
What is EU law about?

In 2014, the internet search company Google was told to remove personal data on a named individual from a list of search results. In 2008, a suspected terrorist succeeded in overturning a measure freezing his assets. In 2005, a German lawyer successfully challenged a contractual clause limiting the duration of his employment because he was over the age of 52.

These cases were controversial. The first, *Google Spain v AEPD*, was seen by some as establishing a so-called 'right to be forgotten'. It pitted privacy campaigners against those who champion the freedom of the internet. The second, *Kadi*, contravened a resolution of the United Nations Security Council adopted under the Charter of the United Nations. It attracted criticism from those who thought that priority should have been given to the UN Charter as well as those concerned by its security implications. The third, *Mangold*, was publicly criticized by a former President of Germany as an unwarranted intrusion into national labour market policy.

A common feature of all these cases is that they were decided by the Court of Justice of the European Union (CJEU) (see Figure 1) and involved the application of European Union (EU) law. This is because they raised issues that the Member States of the EU (currently twenty-eight in number: see Box 1) had decided should

1. Approaching the CJEU.

be regulated in a uniform way at the level of the EU rather than left to each Member State to deal with as it saw fit.

The range of issues that the EU has been given the power to regulate has grown significantly since it was founded by just six Member States in 1951. In that year the Treaty establishing the European Coal and Steel Community (ECSC) was signed in Paris, entering into force in 1952. Part of Europe's efforts to secure an enduring peace after the ravages of two world wars and to restore its economic vitality, the ECSC Treaty established a common market in coal and steel. This was intended to contribute, as Article 2 of the Treaty put it, 'to economic expansion, growth of employment and a rising standard of living in the Member States'. It meant eliminating obstacles to trade in coal and steel between the Member States so that the separate national markets in those products could merge into a single market.

The ECSC Treaty was concluded for a period of fifty years. Although limited in scope, its initial success prompted the

Box 1 The Member States of the EU

Founder members (27 July 1952)
Belgium, France, Germany, Italy, Luxembourg, the Netherlands

1st enlargement (1 January 1973)
Denmark, Ireland, United Kingdom*

2nd enlargement (1 January 1981)
Greece

3rd enlargement (1 January 1986)
Portugal, Spain

4th enlargement (1 January 1995)
Austria, Finland, Sweden

5th enlargement (1 May 2004)
Czech Republic, Cyprus, Estonia, Hungary, Latvia,
Lithuania, Malta, Poland, Slovakia, Slovenia

6th enlargement (1 January 2007)
Bulgaria, Romania

7th enlargement (1 July 2013)
Croatia

*The UK voted to leave the EU in a referendum held on 23 June 2016

Member States to embark on a much more ambitious venture:
the European Economic Community (EEC), established by a
treaty signed in Rome in 1957. Recording the Member States'
determination 'to lay the foundations of an ever closer union
among the peoples of Europe', the EEC Treaty would have a
profound effect on the continent's economics and politics.

Concluded for an unlimited period, the EEC Treaty added a
common market of general scope to that which already existed
in coal and steel. (It absorbed those products when the ECSC
Treaty expired in 2002.) The EEC common market envisaged the

adoption of common policies, notably in the sphere of agriculture and fisheries, and in certain areas the removal of differences between the national laws of the Member States (a process known as the approximation or harmonization of laws). At its heart lay the free movement of goods, persons, services, and capital. These are known as the four freedoms and they remain fundamental to the EU.

The free movement of goods

Among the four freedoms, the free movement of goods between Member States held pride of place. Goods entering the EEC from third countries (that is, non-member States) were required to pay a uniform tariff regardless of their point of entry. Internally a range of obstacles to the free movement of goods between Member States was prohibited. The aim was to create a customs union in which goods could circulate freely.

Member States were not allowed to impose customs duties or other charges having the same effect on imports from other Member States. They were prevented from laying down limits on the quantity of goods that could be imported from other Member States (or quantitative restrictions) and measures which had the same effect. The implications of that prohibition were far-reaching. It was found to have been infringed by Belgian rules requiring margarine to be sold in cube-shaped packaging (*Rau v De Smedt* (1982)). The same fate befell the German *Reinheitsgebot*, or purity requirement, which prevented beer manufactured in other Member States from being sold in Germany if it contained ingredients which were not permitted by German legislation (*Commission v Germany* (1987)).

The EEC Treaty also tackled less direct obstacles to the free movement of goods. In particular, it prevented Member States from protecting their own products indirectly by taxing the products of other Member States more heavily. The UK fell foul of that rule when it was found to be taxing wine imported from other Member States at a higher rate than beer of domestic origin (*Commission v United Kingdom* (1983)). There were also strict controls on the extent to which Member States could grant subsidies (known as State aid) to businesses. In 2016, the EU found that tax benefits of up to €13 billion granted by Ireland to American technology company Apple were incompatible with the rules on State aid because they gave it a competitive advantage over other businesses. Ireland was required to recover the unpaid tax. The EU's decision is being challenged before the CJEU by Ireland and Apple.

The free movement of people

This might all seem rather dry, the stuff of large corporations. However, the common market was not confined to goods and business. It also gave rights to people. Member State nationals were entitled to accept offers of employment in other Member States. In a departure from the strict wording of the Treaty, the CJEU held that Member State nationals were also entitled to move to another Member State and stay there for a reasonable period to look for work (*Antonissen* (1991)). They did not need a visa and could take family members with them, whether or not they were themselves nationals of a Member State. They and the members of their family were given a right to equal treatment with the nationals of the host State. Arrangements were made to ensure that migrant workers could claim social security benefits in the host State and did not lose benefits they had built up in their home State.

Member State nationals were also given a right to establish themselves permanently or provide services temporarily in another Member State under the same conditions as that State's own nationals. The right of establishment was to 'include the right to take up and pursue activities as self-employed persons and to set up and manage undertakings' (Article 52 EEC, now

Article 49 TFEU). Services included activities of an industrial, commercial, or professional character which were 'normally provided for remuneration' (Article 60 EEC, now Article 57 TFEU).

The right to provide services turned out to be broader than might at first sight have been assumed. In a far-reaching decision, the CJEU held that a person *receiving* services had a right to go to the Member State where the person *providing* them was established. The CJEU saw this as a necessary complement to the provider's right to travel to the Member State of the recipient (*Luisi and Carbone v Ministero del Tesoro* (1984)). Beneficiaries of the CJEU's decision included tourists and people seeking medical treatment. In a case involving the sale of financial services by telephone, the CJEU held that the right to provide services in another Member State could apply where neither the provider nor the recipient left their home State (*Alpine Investments* (1995)).

The scope of the free movement rules

Only a small category of tasks—employment in the public service and activities connected with the exercise of official authority—was excluded entirely from the scope of these rights. In *Commission v Belgium* (1980), the CJEU said that this exclusion was limited to posts which presume 'a special relationship of allegiance to the State and reciprocity of rights and duties which form the foundation of the bond of nationality'. The CJEU rejected the argument that it should take account of the way posts were classified under national law. Such a test would be unsatisfactory because it would allow Member States to remove certain functions from the scope of the free movement rules at will.

While the Treaty rules on free movement evidently applied to national restrictions which *discriminated* against goods or people from other Member States, it was initially disputed whether they also covered national measures restricting freedom of movement on a *non-discriminatory* basis. The position was clarified in the 'Cassis de Dijon' case (1979), where the CJEU held that a product lawfully produced and marketed in one Member State could in principle be marketed in any other Member State, even though it might not satisfy the rules applicable there. This showed that discrimination was not relevant to the question whether a national rule amounted to a measure having the same effect as a quantitative restriction. The essential question was whether access to the market had been impeded.

The CJEU's decision resulted in challenges to an increasing range of national rules. An example that became notorious was limits on Sunday trading. These were said to have the same effect as quantitative restrictions because they reduced sales of imported goods by restricting the times when they could be sold, even though domestic goods were affected in exactly the same way (see e.g. *Torfaen Borough Council v B&Q* (1989)).

The CJEU was persuaded to modify its stance in *Keck and Mithouard* (1993). There a distinction was introduced between national rules laying down requirements that the goods themselves had to meet (e.g. on their form, size, weight, composition, or labelling) and those relating to the way they were sold. Rules in the former category were caught by the Treaty whether discriminatory or not. However, rules in the latter category were not caught as long as they applied to all traders and had the same effect on domestic and imported products.

The rules on workers, establishment, and services may also catch non-discriminatory national rules. The *Keck* approach has not been extended to these areas. An important case on workers where non-discriminatory rules were found to be unlawful is *Bosman* (1995), which was to have a profound effect on the organization of professional football in Europe. *Bosman* involved the legality of two rules laid down by football governing bodies.

One required a club wishing to employ a player after his contract with another club had expired to pay that club a transfer fee. The other limited the number of foreign players a club could field.

Previous cases established that, although EU law did not affect rules that were considered to be of purely sporting interest (such as the composition of national teams), it did cover sport where it constituted an economic activity. The CJEU therefore ruled in *Bosman* that the Treaty provisions on workers applied to rules regulating the terms on which professional sports players were employed. It concluded that, as far as EU nationals were concerned, the limit on the number of foreign players that clubs could field was unlawful. The same was true of the transfer rules where they prevented a professional footballer from joining a club in another Member State unless it paid a fee to his former club. This was so even though those rules did not discriminate between players on grounds of nationality. The CJEU's decision radically altered the relationship between professional footballers and their clubs. It helps explain why, if you go to a professional football match between club teams in Europe, the players fielded by each team might all be foreign nationals.

Who is bound by the free movement rules?

In *Bosman*, the football authorities pointed out that the Treaty rules on workers were addressed to Member States. Since they were private bodies, they maintained that those rules did not apply to them. That argument was rejected by the CJEU, which said that the behaviour of private bodies could not be allowed to undermine the obligations of Member States.

The CJEU has taken the same approach in the context of the rules on establishment and services. The leading examples are *Viking* and *Laval* (2007). In the first case, Viking, a ferry operator, wanted to reflag a vessel from the Finnish to the Estonian flag. This would have enabled it to pay wages at Estonian rates, which were lower than Finnish rates. In the second case, Laval, a Latvian company, sent workers from Latvia to Sweden to work on building sites. They were paid at Latvian rates rather than the higher Swedish rates. The conduct of both Viking and Laval led to industrial action against them, which they claimed was unlawful.

The CJEU accepted that the right to take collective action, including the right to strike, was a fundamental right, but ruled that it was qualified by the Treaty rules on establishment and services. Those rules could be used to challenge the actions of trade unions. Industrial action they organized could therefore amount to an unlawful restriction on freedom of movement. These decisions attracted criticism because of their tendency to discourage workers from exercising their fundamental right to take collective action in defence of their interests.

By contrast, the Treaty rules on the free movement of goods do not generally impose obligations on private parties. In *Sapod Audic* (2002), the CJEU said that a provision of a contract agreed between individuals could not be regarded as an infringement of those rules because it was not imposed by a Member State. However, the State may sometimes be held responsible for the conduct of apparently private bodies. An example is the 'Buy Irish' case (1982), where the activities of the Irish Goods Council, a company limited by guarantee, in promoting products made in Ireland were held to be attributable to the Irish government, which appointed its management committee, covered most of its expenses, and influenced its conduct.

Justifying obstacles to freedom of movement

Even the most fervent advocate of free movement would probably accept that there are some circumstances when it is right to restrict it. A product or a person might pose a threat to public health or public safety. A person might not be qualified to pursue a particular activity.

The Treaty recognized this. While it imposed an absolute prohibition on customs charges and charges of equivalent effect, quantitative restrictions and measures having the same effect were treated more leniently. The Treaty said that such measures might be permitted where they were justified on any of the following grounds:

(a) public morality, public policy, or public security;

(b) the protection of health and life of humans, animals, or plants;

(c) the protection of national treasures possessing artistic, historic, or archaeological value;

(d) the protection of industrial and commercial property (i.e. intellectual property rights, such as patents, trade marks, and copyright).

To guard against abuse, the Treaty added that national measures which were justified on any of those grounds must not in any event 'constitute a means of arbitrary discrimination or a disguised restriction on trade between Member States' (Article 36 EEC, now Article 36 TFEU). In other words, they must be specifically designed to safeguard the interest invoked. In the same way, Member States could restrict the rights to work, establish yourself, or provide a service in another Member State on grounds of public policy, public security, or public health.

The Treaty-based justifications have not changed since the EEC Treaty entered into force. Since then the scope of the rules on freedom of movement has become clearer and new values and interests have emerged as worthy of protection. In 'Cassis de Dijon', the CJEU accepted that obstacles to the free movement of goods might be legitimate where they were necessary to satisfy certain overriding interests, such as the enforcement of tax laws, the fairness of commercial transactions, or consumer protection. Later cases have added the protection of interests like working conditions, national culture, the environment, and press diversity.

The CJEU takes a similar approach to the justification of obstacles to the free movement of persons, the right of establishment, and the freedom to provide services (*Gebhard* (1995)).

In order to rely on these various grounds of justification, whether contained in the Treaty or the case law, a Member State must satisfy the principle of proportionality. This requires it to show that the measure concerned is both *suitable* and *necessary* to achieve its objective. This may mean asking whether it imposes an excessive burden on those affected by it. Takis Tridimas of King's College London observes: 'the essential characteristic of the principle is that the Court performs a balancing exercise between the objectives pursued by the measure in issue and its adverse effects on individual freedom'.

What is the relationship between overriding interests and the justifications expressly laid down in the Treaty? One view, based on the CJEU's early case law on goods, is that overriding interests may be invoked only in respect of national restrictions which are *non-discriminatory*. This view gives greater legal weight to the grounds of justification contained in the Treaty than to overriding interests, because it allows the former to be used to justify even discriminatory national obstacles. As Stefan Enchelmaier of the University of Oxford points out, it means that non-discriminatory restrictions are treated more leniently because they are covered by an extended catalogue of justifications.

However, later case law casts doubt on the view that overriding interests are confined to non-discriminatory national restrictions. *Josemans* (2010) concerned an attempt by the Municipality of Maastricht in the Netherlands to prevent people resident in other Member States from travelling to Maastricht to purchase cannabis in coffee shops where the sale of soft drugs was officially tolerated. The CJEU said that the steps taken by the Municipality amounted to a restriction on the freedom of coffee shop owners to provide services and the right of people resident in other Member States to receive them. However, those steps were 'justified by the objective of combating drug tourism and the accompanying public nuisance'. Although they were clearly discriminatory, the CJEU's decision was not based on the justifications expressly laid down in the Treaty.

Whether or not overriding interests may be used to justify discriminatory national rules, could it not be said that the CJEU acted improperly in effectively recognizing justifications that the Member States had not themselves agreed to when they signed the Treaty? This would amount to a claim that the CJEU was guilty of *judicial activism*, in other words of straying outside its remit. This is a claim that is often levelled at the CJEU. In this context, it would not be entirely fanciful. However, the Member States had many opportunities after 'Cassis de Dijon' to amend the Treaty to reverse the effect of that case. Their failure to do so suggests that they were broadly happy with the outcome.

The free movement of capital

The fourth freedom, the free movement of capital, was closely linked not only to the common market but also to an aspiration that came to the fore only after the EEC Treaty was signed, that of economic and monetary union (EMU). Broadly speaking, the term capital refers to financial assets which can be invested to generate wealth. The Treaty rules on capital were originally somewhat tame, but were reinforced in the early 1990s. They now prohibit all restrictions on the movement of capital between Member States. Unlike other Treaty rules on freedom of movement, those on capital also prohibit restrictions between Member States and third countries. The Treaty goes on to set out certain grounds on which restrictions may be justified.

Where national regulatory obstacles to the free movement of capital are challenged, the Court takes its usual approach to obstacles to freedom of movement. It does not require discrimination to be shown and interprets the grounds of justification narrowly, requiring the principle of proportionality to be satisfied. *Commission v United Kingdom* (2003) concerned the privatization of the British Airports Authority. The British government had retained a so-called 'golden share' in the privatized company, restricting the ability of other shareholders to participate in its management and acquire voting rights. The United Kingdom argued that these arrangements were lawful because they applied to all Member State nationals without discrimination on grounds of nationality and did not restrict access to the market. However, the Court disagreed, pointing out that access to the market was affected because the golden share was 'liable to deter investors from other Member States' from acquiring shares in the company.

In the tax field, the Court has taken a more lenient approach, being prepared to tolerate international double taxation. In *Kerckhaert* (2006), for example, it held that the charging by Belgium of tax on dividends paid by a French company without deducting tax already levied in France was compatible with the rules on the free movement of capital. This was so even though the effect was to tax the dividends paid by the French company more heavily than dividends paid by a Belgian company, thereby discouraging investment in French companies by people resident in Belgium. According to the Court, the Belgian tax legislation did not make any distinction 'between dividends from companies established in Belgium and dividends from companies established in another Member State'. Any adverse consequences for taxpayers resulted from 'the exercise in parallel by two Member States of their fiscal sovereignty'.

In cases involving third countries, the Court has accepted that Member States may be able to justify restrictions on capital movements for reasons that would not justify restrictions on such movements between Member States (*FII Group Litigation* (2006)). Jukka Snell of the University of Turku, Finland, observes:

'the extra-EU aspect of the free movement of capital remains the least explored area of the four freedoms, and may well result in significant tensions...'

Competition

It was not just government action that threatened the free movement of goods and services. Agreements between businesses could pose a similar threat if, for example, they agreed not to compete with each other in their respective national markets. The EEC Treaty therefore aimed to ensure that competition in the common market was not distorted. Insofar as trade between Member States was affected, private agreements restricting or distorting competition as well as abuses of market power were prohibited.

This led to an initial focus on agreements between businesses at different levels of the distribution chain (so-called vertical agreements), such as manufacturers and wholesalers or wholesalers and retailers. These were considered particularly likely to threaten market integration (*Consten and Grundig v Commission* (1966)).

As the common market matured, the focus switched to agreements between competitors (so-called horizontal agreements) and the need to control market power in order to promote efficiency and protect the interests of consumers. This change of emphasis was reflected in the EU's allegation in April 2016 that Google had abused its market power through its Android operating system and its relationship with manufacturers of smartphones and tablet computers.

In 1989, special rules were introduced to block mergers and takeovers which would significantly impede effective competition in the common market. In May 2016, those rules were used to block a deal that would have reduced the number of mobile phone network operators in the UK from four to three due to concerns about higher prices and reduced innovation.

Social policy

When the EEC Treaty was signed, many believed that the common market would automatically lead to better living standards and working conditions. The Treaty's social provisions were therefore limited, but one stood out. Article 119 EEC (now Article 257 TFEU) laid down the principle of equal pay for men and women. It was designed to avoid a 'race to the bottom', in which Member States which already had rules on equal pay were forced to dilute them in order to compete with Member States which did not. In the seminal *Defrenne II* case (1976), the CJEU declared that 'the principle of equal pay forms part of the foundations of the Community'. It later went further, acknowledging that the economic aim of the principle was secondary to its social aim, which constituted 'the expression of a fundamental human right' (*Deutsche Telekom v Schröder* (2000)).

A growing realization that better working conditions could not simply be left to the common market led to increased emphasis on social policy in the Treaties. The EU is now required to 'work for … a highly competitive social market economy, aiming at full employment and social progress …' (Article 3(3) TEU). The EU may also take action 'to combat discrimination based on sex, racial or ethnic origin, religion or belief, disability, age or sexual orientation' (Article 19 TFEU). That provision, introduced in 1999 by the Treaty of Amsterdam, lay behind the *Mangold* case, mentioned at the beginning of this chapter.

The transitional period

It would not have been feasible for the common market to be established overnight: the Member States and their economies needed time to adapt. The EEC Treaty therefore said that the common market should be established gradually over a transitional period comprising three stages, the last of which ended on 31 December 1969.

Chapter 2
From Common Market to European Union

When the transitional period expired, the common market was
still far from complete. By the mid-1980s, however, it began to
seem politically feasible to bring it to fruition. In February 1986,
the Member States signed a new treaty called the Single European
Act (SEA) committing them to establishing what was now to be
called the *internal* market by the end of 1992. The SEA defined
the internal market as 'an area without internal frontiers in which
the free movement of goods, persons, services and capital is
ensured...' By the end of 1992 a great deal of progress had been
made, although more still remains to be done on services, energy,
and the digital economy.

At the same time, the Member States began to explore widening
the remit of the EEC to embrace additional policy areas. The SEA
introduced new provisions on the health and safety of workers. It
required action to be taken to reduce regional disparities in the
EEC, making use of the so-called structural funds, such as the
European Regional Development Fund and the European Social
Fund. It introduced powers for the EEC to act to protect the
environment. Such action was to be based on three principles:
that preventive action should be taken; that environmental
damage should be rectified at source; and that the polluter
should pay. The need to protect the environment was
henceforward to be a component of the EEC's other policies.

In the 1970s, the Member States had agreed to work towards the establishment of EMU. They also began to cooperate informally in the areas of foreign policy and counter-terrorism. The SEA inserted new provisions for EMU into the EEC Treaty. It also contained a free-standing section on foreign policy cooperation. (This explains the curious title of the SEA: although containing amendments to the Community Treaties alongside provisions on foreign policy cooperation which were legally separate from those Treaties, it was a single act.)

A leap forward in all three areas—EMU, foreign policy, and crime prevention generally—was taken in 1992. In that year, against the backdrop of the collapse of communism in eastern Europe, the Treaty on European Union (TEU) was signed in Maastricht, giving birth to a new legal entity: the EU. The TEU laid down detailed provisions for the introduction of a single European currency, later baptized the euro. (I discuss the difficulties to which this would give rise in Chapter 9.) In addition, the TEU gave the EEC (renamed the EC: European Community) new responsibilities in a range of areas. These included culture, public health, consumer protection, 'trans-European networks' (large infrastructure networks in the areas of transport, telecommunications, and energy), research and technological development, and policy towards developing countries. It also introduced new provisions under the umbrella of the EU (but technically outside the scope of the *Community* Treaties) on a Common Foreign and Security Policy (CFSP) and justice and home affairs. These came to be known respectively as the second and third pillars of the EU. They initially involved a less advanced form of integration than the first pillar, to which the ECSC and EC Treaties belonged.

Furthermore, the TEU granted 'citizenship of the Union' to everyone who was a national of a Member State. A complement to national citizenship, EU citizenship initially seemed to be a portmanteau notion comprising mainly rights already enjoyed by Member State nationals under the Treaties. However, the CJEU later declared it 'destined to become the fundamental status of nationals of the Member States...' (*Grzelczyk* (2001)). Unlike the provisions on the free movement of persons, citizenship was found to give such nationals a right to move and reside within the territory of the Member States even if they were not economically active (*Baumbast and R* (2002); *Zhu and Chen v Secretary of State* (2004)).

However, the CJEU later rowed back, holding that the Treaty precluded only national measures depriving EU citizens of what it called 'the genuine enjoyment of the substance of the rights' conferred on them (*Ruiz Zambrano* (2011)). The hint of retrenchment continued in *Dano* (2014), where the CJEU limited the right of economically inactive EU citizens to claim welfare benefits in Member States other than their own. This seemed to be a response to unease about 'welfare tourism', the idea that people might be induced to move to Member States offering the most generous welfare benefits.

The contemporary EU

The Treaty of Lisbon abolished the pillar structure along with the term 'European Community'. The new European Union was to be a single entity based on two Treaties each of equal status: a revised TEU and a Treaty on the Functioning of the European Union (TFEU), essentially a revised EC Treaty (see Box 2). This brought the provisions of the TEU on foreign policy and justice and home affairs under the same roof as the areas which formerly fell within the jurisdiction of the EC.

In the case of the foreign policy provisions, their distinctive character was retained. The provisions on justice and home affairs were treated differently. Those provisions, along with the Schengen Agreements on the abolition of internal border checks signed by only some of the Member States in 1985 and 1990, had been brought partly within the remit of the Community by the

Box 2 Some of the main EU Treaties

Treaty	Signature	Entry into Force
ECSC Treaty	18 April 1951	23 July 1952 (expired 23 July 2002)
EEC Treaty	25 March 1957	1 January 1958
Single European Act	17 and 28 February 1986	1 July 1987
Treaty of Maastricht	7 February 1992	1 November 1993
Treaty of Amsterdam	2 October 1997	1 May 1999
Treaty of Nice	26 February 2001	1 February 2003
Constitutional Treaty	29 October 2004	Did not enter into force
Treaty of Lisbon	13 December 2007	1 December 2009

Treaty of Amsterdam. There the phrase 'area of freedom, security and justice' (AFSJ) was coined to capture the EU's ambitions in this field. The process was taken a stage further at Lisbon, when the AFSJ took its place alongside freedom of movement, competition, and other matters at the very heart of the TFEU.

The Area of Freedom, Security, and Justice

The AFSJ is one of the most significant and contentious extensions of the EU's jurisdiction since its inception as the EEC (see Box 3). There are two main reasons for this. One is that it impinges on matters that belong to the very core of what it means to be a sovereign State. The other is that it requires a

Box 3 Article 67 TFEU

1. The Union shall constitute an area of freedom, security and justice with respect for fundamental rights and the different legal systems and traditions of the Member States.

2. It shall ensure the absence of internal border controls for persons and shall frame a common policy on asylum, immigration and external border control, based on solidarity between Member States, which is fair towards third-country nationals. For the purpose of this Title [i.e. sub-division of the Treaty], stateless persons shall be treated as third-country nationals.

3. The Union shall endeavour to ensure a high level of security through measures to prevent and combat crime, racism and xenophobia, and through measures for coordination and cooperation between police and judicial authorities and other competent authorities, as well as through the mutual recognition of judgments in criminal matters and, if necessary, through the approximation of criminal laws.

4. The Union shall facilitate access to justice, in particular through the principle of mutual recognition of judicial and extrajudicial decisions in civil matters.

balance to be struck between security and the fundamental rights of individuals. To allay concerns among some Member States about the likely approach of the CJEU, the AFSJ was not brought fully within its jurisdiction until 30 November 2014, five years after the Lisbon Treaty entered into force. Even that was not enough to satisfy the UK and Ireland (between which there are special travel arrangements of long standing) or Denmark, which were the subject of further exemptions.

The AFSJ provides the EU with a legal framework for responding to the huge challenges posed by the global movement of people fleeing conflict, the consequences of climate change, or searching for a better life. A common visa policy has been adopted and an agency known as Frontex established to assist Member States in the territory covered by the Schengen Agreements (known as the Schengen area) with the management of their external borders. There are also rules on refugees and irregular (or illegal) immigration. These include measures on expulsion and people trafficking and on penalizing those who employ or assist in the transportation of irregular migrants. The provisions of the AFSJ in this area were stretched to breaking point by the migration crisis that erupted in 2015. I will return to this in Chapter 9.

The other main component of the AFSJ is judicial and police cooperation in criminal matters. The EU's best-known initiative here is probably the European Arrest Warrant (EAW), which enables a court in one Member State to secure the rapid apprehension and surrender of a suspect who has fled to another Member State. Established in 2002 under the pre-Lisbon version of the TEU, the EAW is much more effective in recovering suspected offenders than the extradition arrangements previously in place.

An EAW was used to secure the swift return to France of Salah Abdeslam, who was suspected of involvement in the 2015 Paris attacks. He was arrested in Brussels on 18 March 2016, where further acts of terrorism were carried out just four days later. He was transferred to Paris on 27 April 2016. Before the EAW, it took ten years to extradite another terrorist, Rachid Ramda, from the UK to France. An EAW issued in 2010 by a Swedish prosecutor in respect of WikiLeaks co-founder Julian Assange attracted a blaze of publicity. Then in England, Assange was wanted in Sweden in connection with rape allegations. A challenge by Assange to the validity of the EAW in the English courts was unsuccessful and he managed to avoid returning to Sweden only by seeking refuge in the Ecuadorean Embassy in London.

The EAW heightened concerns about the conditions in which suspects were sometimes held in custody. In *Aranyosi and Căldăraru* (2016), the CJEU held that there was an absolute prohibition on inhuman or degrading treatment in EU law. A court asked to execute an EAW could therefore decline to do so if convinced that there was a real risk that an individual would otherwise be exposed to such treatment.

In 1999, a body called Europol was created to support

> action by the Member States' police authorities and other law enforcement services and their mutual cooperation in preventing and combating serious crime affecting two or more Member States, terrorism and forms of crime which affect a common interest covered by a Union policy.   (Article 88(1) TFEU)

Europol can only take operational action in conjunction with national authorities and has no power to use 'coercive measures'.

Europol was reinforced in 2002 by the establishment of Eurojust under the pre-Lisbon TEU. The task of Eurojust is to promote 'coordination and cooperation between national investigating and prosecuting authorities in relation to serious crime affecting two or more Member States or requiring a prosecution on common bases...' (Article 85(1) TFEU).

The TFEU also provides for the creation of a European Public Prosecutor's Office (EPPO). The EPPO would be 'responsible for investigating, prosecuting and bringing to judgment, where appropriate in liaison with Europol, the perpetrators of, and accomplices in, offences against the Union's financial interests...' (Article 86(2) TFEU). There is provision for the powers of the EPPO to be extended to include 'serious crime having a cross-border dimension...' (Article 86(4) TFEU). The EPPO would prosecute any such offence in the courts of the Member State where it was alleged to have taken place. It would reinforce the European Anti-Fraud Office known as OLAF (after its French name), which relies on the Member States to prosecute any fraud it uncovers.

Steve Peers of the University of Essex has questioned the need for an EPPO but the utility of these other initiatives is widely acknowledged. It was sometimes objected that EU action in this field would threaten the UK's common law tradition and might lead to an EU criminal code. Both objections were rejected by the House of Lords EU Committee, which said in a report published in 2013 that 'none of the pre-Lisbon police and criminal justice measures undermines the UK's common law systems in any way' and described concerns about 'the possible development of a pan-EU criminal code' as 'misplaced'. It observed that no Member State could hope to assure its internal security or the enforcement of the rule of law without cross-border cooperation on policing and criminal justice matters.

Nonetheless, special arrangements have been made for some Member States. The UK and Ireland were authorized to maintain the Common Travel Area, under which the movement of people between their respective territories is regulated. Both countries were granted opt-outs from the AFSJ, though they were permitted to opt in to particular measures, either before or after their adoption. They were granted opt-outs from the Schengen *acquis*, the body of law based on the Schengen Agreements. They were permitted to take part in some or all of the *acquis*, but only with the permission of the other Member States. This has occasionally led to litigation, with the CJEU generally siding with the other Member States where permission has been refused.

Ireland was less suspicious of EU activity in this area than the UK. Ireland was authorized to withdraw from its opt-out from the AFSJ and participate in full. By contrast, the UK alone had an additional right to opt out of all AFSJ measures adopted before the entry into force of the Lisbon Treaty so that it could avoid the extension of the CJEU's jurisdiction over such measures on 1 December 2014.

The legal hokey cokey continued, for the UK then had the right to opt back in to measures which it wished to continue to apply to it despite the CJEU's enlarged powers. The House of Lords EU Committee advised the UK Government against exercising the opt-out, which it said would have 'significant adverse negative repercussions for the internal security of the United Kingdom and the administration of criminal justice in the United Kingdom'. That advice was not followed and the opt-out was exercised. The list of measures to which the UK opted back in—which included the EAW—proved politically contentious.

Special rules have also been made to accommodate Denmark, which has an opt-out from the AFSJ. It is entitled to opt in to individual measures building on the Schengen *acquis*. Where it does so, however, such measures create obligations between Denmark and the other Member States involved which are binding under international law rather than EU law, which would be more stringent. In a referendum on 3 December 2015, the Danes rejected a proposal to align themselves more closely with the AFSJ.

While some Member States have opted out, certain non-member States have opted in. Denmark and the two other Nordic Member States, Sweden and Finland, share a passport union with Norway and Iceland, which are outside the EU. To preserve their passport union, all five States signed an agreement in 1999 extending the Schengen area to Norway and Iceland. Agreements have also been signed extending the Schengen area to Switzerland and Liechtenstein.

Competence creep?

The seemingly inexorable growth in the EU's remit—sometimes called 'competence creep'—has not been universally welcomed.

Some see it as inherent in 'the process of creating an ever closer union among the peoples of Europe' (Article 1 TEU). Others say that the EU should now relinquish some of its powers. Against that background, the British Government launched a review in July 2012 of the balance of powers between the UK and the EU. The then Prime Minister, David Cameron, mentioned the review in his Bloomberg speech of 23 January 2013, when he announced his intention to negotiate a new settlement for the UK with the rest of the EU and to put the result to a referendum of the British people.

The review was completed in December 2014, by which time thirty-two detailed reports had been published. Lord Hannay, a former British Permanent Representative (or ambassador) to the EU, was quoted in *The Observer* on 28 March 2015 as saying: 'The single, clear message from the review is that in none of its 32 chapters is there a compelling case for the repatriation of powers from Brussels to Westminster and Whitehall.'

Chapter 3
Secondary EU law

Of the rules I've mentioned so far, not all are actually contained in the Treaties themselves. A novel feature of the Treaties was that they created institutions distinct from the Member States with the capacity to make law. Such law is known as the secondary law of the EU. It is subordinate to the Treaties, which belong to the primary law of the EU. Some of the rules I referred to in Chapters 1 and 2 belong to the EU's primary law, some to its secondary law.

Conferral and competence

The capacity of the EU's institutions to make law is not unlimited. This is because the EU is based on a principle called conferral. That principle plays an important role in preserving a balance between the powers of the EU and those of the Member States. It helps ensure that the institutions do not make law willy-nilly, but only where they are given express or implied powers to do so by the Treaties.

According to Article 5(2) TEU:

> Under the principle of conferral, the Union shall act only within the limits of the competences conferred upon it by the Member States in the Treaties to attain the objectives set out therein. Competences

not conferred upon the Union in the Treaties remain with the Member States.

This is reinforced by Article 13 (2) TEU, which says that '[e]ach institution shall act within the limits of the powers conferred upon it in the Treaties, and in conformity with the procedures, conditions and objectives set out in them…'. That provision reflects another important principle, that of institutional balance, which requires the institutions to exercise their powers 'with due regard for the powers of the other institutions' (*Council v Commission* (2015)).

A provision of the Treaties which gives the institutions a 'competence'—or law-making power—is known as a legal basis. Such provisions specify the scope of the competence conferred and how and by whom it may be exercised. The EU's competences fall into three categories.

The most extensive powers are those which give the EU exclusive competence in a given area. In such areas, the Member States may legislate only if permitted to do so by the EU or to implement EU measures. Article 3 TFEU lists the following areas as falling within the EU's exclusive competence:

(a) customs union;
(b) the competition rules necessary for the functioning of the internal market;
(c) monetary policy for the Member States whose currency is the euro;
(d) the conservation of marine biological resources under the common fisheries policy;
(e) common commercial policy (which concerns trade with third countries).

The EU also has exclusive competence to enter into certain forms of international agreement.

At the other end of the scale are areas where the EU has competence to 'support, coordinate or supplement the actions of the Member States'. Article 6 TFEU lists the areas concerned as follows:

(a) protection and improvement of human health;
(b) industry;
(c) culture;
(d) tourism;
(e) education, vocational training, youth, and sport;
(f) civil protection;
(g) administrative cooperation.

Between those two extremes lie several areas where the EU shares competence with the Member States. This means that both may legislate, although the Member States are only permitted to do so to the extent that the EU has not. If the EU decides to stop acting, the Member States regain their competence to do so. The main areas where the EU shares competence with the Member States are listed in Article 4(2) TFEU as follows:

(a) internal market;
(b) aspects of social policy;
(c) economic, social, and territorial cohesion (i.e. reducing regional disparities in the EU);
(d) agriculture and fisheries, excluding the conservation of marine biological resources;
(e) environment;
(f) consumer protection;
(g) transport;
(h) trans-European networks;
(i) energy;

(j) area of freedom, security, and justice;

(k) common safety concerns in public health matters.

There are two areas where the exercise by the EU of its competence does not prevent the Member States from exercising theirs:
(i) research, technological development, and space; and
(ii) development cooperation and humanitarian aid.

When exercising its law-making powers, the EU has at its disposal the instruments listed in Article 288 TFEU.

The most powerful are *regulations*. These are of general application and are 'binding in their entirety and directly applicable in all Member States'. They impose common requirements on everyone falling within their scope and take effect on their own terms as soon as they are adopted. They are good at achieving uniformity but somewhat inflexible.

Regulations may be contrasted with *directives*. These are addressed to some or all of the Member States and require them to achieve a specified result within a given deadline. Crucially they 'leave to the national authorities the choice of form and methods'. Directives have been particularly important in eliminating disparities between national laws that might undermine the internal market and were used extensively to achieve the objectives of the SEA. They enable Member States to achieve the required result in a way which best suits national laws and practices. They offer more flexibility than regulations but are less effective at achieving uniformity because they rely on further action by the Member States.

A third category of instrument is *decisions*, which are binding in their entirety. They may specify those to whom they are addressed. Where they do so, they are binding only on their addressees. The institutions may also issue *recommendations* and *opinions*, but these have no binding force.

A leading role is played in the exercise of the EU's competences by its four main political institutions: the European Parliament; the European Council; the Council; and the Commission (see Figure 2).

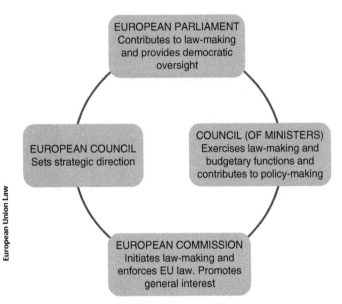

2. **The main political institutions of the EU.**

The European Parliament

The European Parliament is based in Strasbourg, France, but conducts some of its work in Brussels and Luxembourg. It comprises representatives of the EU's citizens. Known as Members of the European Parliament (MEPs), they have been directly elected since 1979, elections taking place across the EU every five years. The total number of MEPs may not exceed 750 in number plus the Parliament's President, who is elected from among its members. Representation is described by Article 14(2)

TEU as 'degressively proportional, with a minimum threshold of six members per Member State'. Currently Cyprus, Estonia, Luxembourg, and Malta have six while Germany has ninety-six (the maximum permitted). Since Germany is so much more populous, an MEP from that State represents many more voters than an MEP from Malta.

MEPs sit in groups reflecting their political affiliation rather than nationality, although they occasionally vote along national lines. The largest group is currently the centre-right European People's Party with 215 seats. The smallest is the Europe of Nations and Freedom Group, whose thirty-nine members include Marine Le Pen, the President of the French *Front National*.

The role of the European Parliament was originally described by the EEC Treaty as 'advisory and supervisory' (Article 137 EEC), but its powers have grown significantly over the years. It now exercises considerable influence and is in many areas of EU competence a co-legislator with the Council. It also sets up Committees of Inquiry (Article 226 TFEU); receives petitions from individuals (Article 227 TFEU); elects the European Ombudsman, who deals with complaints of maladministration by the EU (Article 228 TFEU); and puts formal questions to the Commission, to which the latter is bound to reply (Article 230 TFEU).

The European Council

Meetings of the European Council, often called 'EU summits', take place in Brussels. The European Council consists principally of the Heads of State or Government (HoSG) of the Member States. This cumbersome term accommodates Member States such as France, whose Heads of State have executive responsibilities. Most Member States are represented by their Prime Ministers. National representatives are joined by the President of the Commission and the President of the European Council, who is elected by the HoSG for a term of two and a half years, which may be renewed once. The President of the European Council may not hold a national office (Article 15(6) TEU).

The European Council is intended to 'provide the Union with the necessary impetus for its development' and to set its 'general political directions and priorities'. It normally takes decisions by consensus (Article 15(4) TEU). When it decides by vote, its President and the President of the Commission do not take part (Article 235(1) TFEU).

The task of the President, a post created by the Treaty of Lisbon, is to manage the business of the European Council and chair its meetings. The first President, the Belgian politician Herman Van Rompuy, was famously described by the then UKIP leader Nigel Farage as having 'the charisma of a damp rag and the appearance of a low grade bank clerk'. However, he proved to be a skilled and effective incumbent during an exceptionally difficult period which included the start of the eurozone crisis. He was replaced after two terms by Donald Tusk, a former Prime Minister of Poland, on 1 December 2014. The President of the European Council is now the answer to Henry Kissinger's famous question about who to call when you want to speak to Europe.

The Council

The Council is located in Brussels. It consists of a government minister from each Member State. Its precise composition varies according to the subject it is meeting to discuss. An attempt is made to minimize sticking points ahead of meetings by the Committee of Permanent Representatives (COREPER), a powerful body consisting of the Member States' ambassadors to the EU and their deputies. Council meetings are (with one exception) chaired by the Member State holding the presidency of the Council. This rotates among the Member States every six months following the order laid down in a decision of the European Council, with which the Council (of Ministers) should not be confused!

The exception is the Foreign Affairs Council, which is chaired by the High Representative of the Union for Foreign Affairs and Security Policy, a role created at Lisbon. Appointed by the European Council with the agreement of the President of the Commission, the High Representative conducts the CFSP with the assistance of the EU's diplomatic service, the European External Action Service (EEAS: see Article 27(3) TEU). The High Representative is also a Vice-President of the Commission. The first incumbent, Catherine Ashton, was succeeded on 1 November 2014 by Federica Mogherini, formerly Italian Minister of Foreign Affairs.

Crucial to the functioning of the Council is the way it votes. The EEC Treaty envisaged that it would normally act either unanimously or by qualified majority vote (QMV).

Article 238(4) TFEU provides that abstentions by members 'present in person or represented' do not prevent the Council from acting unanimously. This means that all Member States must be present or represented for a decision requiring unanimity to be taken.

Where QMV applies, the number of votes attributed to Member States was originally weighted broadly according to their populations. To balance the interests of States with widely varying populations, small and medium-sized ones had more votes per capita than large ones. To attain a qualified majority, a specified threshold of votes had to be reached. The threshold meant that no single Member State could hold things up and encouraged the formation of alliances, either to approve or to block a proposal. Once adopted a measure would apply to all Member States entitled to vote.

In a number of important areas of Community competence, QMV was introduced progressively during the course of the transitional period. However, as the start of the third stage on 1 January 1966 approached, the Community was plunged into crisis by France, whose President, Charles de Gaulle, objected to the planned expansion in the use of QMV and the growing influence of the

Commission. The attitude of de Gaulle chimes with contemporary euroscepticism. QMV permits dissident Member States to be outvoted and the Commission is able to act independently of national governments. In the last six months of 1965, France pressed home its concerns by adopting an 'empty chair policy', refusing to participate in Council meetings and thereby blocking decisions requiring unanimity.

The crisis was brought to an end by the so-called Luxembourg Compromise of January 1966. This informal agreement came to be interpreted as granting Member States a power of veto in the Council whenever they considered their vital national interests to be at stake. Although the Luxembourg Compromise was rarely invoked directly, it led the Council to seek a consensus on all draft legislation even where unanimity was not required by the Treaty. This practice had the effect of delaying the adoption of legislation and diluting its content. It posed a serious threat to the achievement of the Community's objectives and was a major factor in its failure to complete the common market by the end of the transitional period on 31 December 1969.

The early 1980s saw a gradual erosion of the practice of consensus. Its demise was confirmed by the SEA. To facilitate the adoption of the measures necessary to complete the internal market by the end of 1992, the SEA made increased provision for the use of QMV. Particularly important was a new Article 100a EEC (now Article 114 TFEU), which for the first time permitted the adoption by QMV of measures to harmonize national laws. The SEA had the effect of cementing the use of QMV wherever possible and necessary. Whether the Luxembourg Compromise can still be invoked is a political rather than a legal question. Since it had no legal status, it has never been formally revoked.

As small and medium-sized Member States became more numerous with successive enlargements, the bias in the QMV system in their favour became more pronounced. Concerns grew that, if the original system were simply extrapolated, it would be possible in an EU of twenty-eight for legislation to be adopted by governments representing less than 50 per cent of the EU's population.

The system was therefore altered by Article 16(4) TEU, which provides:

> As from 1 November 2014, a qualified majority shall be defined as at least 55% of the members of the Council, comprising at least fifteen of them and representing Member States comprising at least 65% of the population of the Union.

This means that qualified majority decisions cannot be taken by a minority of the Member States, however large their populations. To prevent three larger Member States from blocking a qualified majority decision, Article 16(4) adds: 'A blocking minority must include at least four Council members, failing which the qualified majority shall be deemed attained.'

Poland and Spain considered this system less favourable to them than the previous system of weighted votes and managed to extract certain concessions. First, there was a delay before the new system took effect. Secondly, until 31 March 2017 any Council member could request that the old system be used instead of the new one whenever an act was to be adopted by QMV. Thirdly, from 1 November 2014, where a certain proportion of the Member States necessary to constitute a blocking minority opposes the adoption of an act by QMV, the Council must make a further attempt to find broader agreement.

QMV is now the default rule for voting in the Council (Article 16(3) TEU). It is necessary to enable the EU to function effectively. Member States accept it because they calculate that the benefits of EU membership outweigh the risk that they may sometimes find themselves bound by an act they did not support. The fine-tuning the system has undergone shows, however, that the concerns that led to the empty chair crisis of 1965 have not entirely dissipated.

The procedure that must be used for the adoption of an act, including the way the Council must vote, is determined by the act's legal basis. Member States that are opposed to the act may challenge it before the CJEU on the ground that it should have been founded on a different legal basis, one that would have offered the applicant greater safeguards (see Box 4).

(see Box 4)

Box 4 Challenging the legal basis of an act

United Kingdom v Council (1996) concerned the so-called Working Time Directive, which regulates things like annual leave, rest breaks, and weekly working time. It was originally adopted under Article 118a EC by QMV against the wishes of the UK, which challenged its validity before the CJEU. The essence of the UK's claim was that Article 118a did not permit such measures and that it ought to have been adopted under Article 100 EC, which required unanimity in the Council. Article 118a authorized the adoption of directives with the objective of 'encouraging improvements, especially in the working environment, as regards the health and safety of workers...'. The UK maintained that Article 100 was the correct legal basis for measures 'relating to the rights and interests of employed persons'.

The CJEU rejected that argument. There was nothing in the wording of Article 118a, it said, to suggest that it was confined to physical conditions and risks in the workplace. On the contrary, it should be interpreted 'as embracing all factors, physical or otherwise, capable of affecting the health and safety of the worker in his working environment, including in particular certain aspects of the organization of working time'. The CJEU's ruling attracted criticism, but this often seemed to be based more on the policy pursued by the directive than

European Union Law

its legality. As the CJEU pointed out, 'it is not the function of the Court to review the expediency of measures adopted by the legislature'.

The 'Working Time Directive' case may be contrasted with the 'Tobacco Advertising' case (2000), where Germany challenged the validity of a directive on the advertising of tobacco. The directive was based on Article 100a EC, which authorized the adoption by QMV of measures to iron out differences between national laws affecting the establishment and functioning of the internal market. The CJEU said that a measure based on Article 100a had to be genuinely concerned with improving the establishment and functioning of the internal market. It was not enough to show a merely abstract risk that disparities between national rules might constitute obstacles to free movement or distortions of competition. The CJEU concluded that the directive did not satisfy that test and it was therefore quashed.

The Commission

The Commission is located in Brussels, though some of its departments are based in Luxembourg. It is sometimes known as 'the guardian of the Treaties' and plays a pivotal role in the life of the EU. It is required to 'promote the general interest of the Union and take appropriate initiatives to that end' (Article 17(1) TEU). Its main tasks include initiating the EU's law-making processes, making sure that EU law is properly implemented and applied, negotiating agreements between the EU and third countries or international organizations under the supervision of the Council, and implementing the EU's budget.

Like the European Parliament, the Commission serves a term of five years. It is led by a so-called College of twenty-eight Commissioners, one from each Member State. They are supported by a staff of about 33,000 officials. Although Commissioners are often seen as representatives of their countries of origin, the Commission is required to be 'completely independent' and must 'neither seek nor take instructions from any Government or other institution, body, office or entity' (Article 17(3) TEU).

The College is headed by a President, who assigns responsibility for specific policy areas to each Commissioner and may reshuffle responsibilities during the Commission's term of office. He or she may appoint additional Vice-Presidents from among the Commissioners. The President may also require any Commissioner except one to resign. The exception is the High Representative, whose term of office can be terminated only by the European Council, although the Commission President must agree.

The process for appointing the Commission has been altered on several occasions, most recently at Lisbon, and has become very elaborate (see Figure 3). The main result of the changes has been to enhance the role of the European Parliament, which exploited its powers to striking effect when the Commission which entered into office on 1 November 2014 was appointed.

The first step is for the European Council, acting by a qualified majority, to propose a candidate for President to the European Parliament for election. If the proposed candidate is rejected by the Parliament, the European Council must propose a new candidate. The European Council is required to take account of the latest elections to the European Parliament and hold appropriate consultations.

In the run-up to the European parliamentary elections of 2014, the political groups in the Parliament nominated specific individuals (known as *Spitzenkandidaten*, or lead candidates) as their candidates for the presidency of the Commission. After the 2014 elections had taken place, the outgoing Parliament declared that the candidate for the presidency of the Commission proposed by the European Council should be the person chosen by

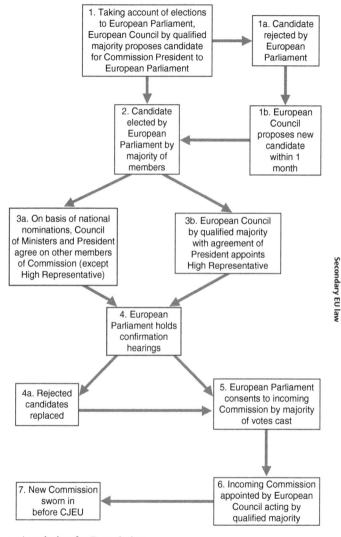

3. Appointing the Commission.

the largest parliamentary group in the incoming Parliament, which most group leaders had agreed to back.

That person turned out to be Jean-Claude Juncker, who was Prime Minister of Luxembourg from 1995 to 2013 and that country's Finance Minister from 1989 to 2009. Unwilling to countenance a prolonged stand-off with the Parliament and voting by qualified majority for the first time, all the HoSG except those from Hungary and the UK eventually endorsed Juncker. He was then elected by the Parliament. On meeting Juncker for the first time after he had entered into office, the then British Prime Minister David Cameron suffered the indignity of being greeted by a high five.

Once the incoming President has been chosen, he or she agrees with the Council of Ministers on the other members. They are chosen from national nominees on the grounds of competence, independence, and 'European commitment' (Article 17(3) TEU). Once this has been done, the entire Commission, including the President and the High Representative, must be approved by the European Parliament, which holds confirmation hearings at which the prospective Commissioners are subjected to robust questioning. In 2004, this led to the replacement of the Italian nominee, Rocco Buttiglione, after he made unguarded remarks about homosexuals and women. The final step is for the Commission to be formally appointed by the European Council.

The *Spitzenkandidaten* process has no legal status. Some say that it has strengthened the Commission's legitimacy, others that it has compromised its independence. Certainly, the Juncker Commission seems closer to the Parliament than some of its predecessors. However, the robustness of the process was soon called into question when Juncker became embroiled in the so-called LuxLeaks scandal, in which leaked documents covering the period 2002–10 revealed that Luxembourg had become a tax haven for multinational companies. In October 2015, the Commission adopted a decision finding that a ruling of the Luxembourg tax authorities in 2012 in respect of Fiat contravened the Treaty rules on State aid by reducing the amount of tax it would otherwise have had to pay. Luxembourg was required to recover the unpaid tax. In June 2016, two whistleblowers involved in the leaks were convicted of theft by a court in Luxembourg and given suspended sentences.

New Commissioners give a solemn undertaking before the CJEU to respect their obligations and behave with integrity and discretion (see Figure 4). If the Council of Ministers or the Commission considers that a Commissioner 'no longer fulfils the conditions required for the performance of his duties' or is 'guilty of serious misconduct', they can apply to the CJEU for him or her to be compulsorily retired or deprived of a pension or other benefits (Articles 245 and 247 TFEU).

Secondary EU law

4. Solemn undertaking given by the President and members of the Barroso Commission before the CJEU (3 May 2010).

The first misconduct case against a Commissioner to result in a judgment of the CJEU was *Commission v Cresson* (2006), where the CJEU said that Commissioners were 'under an obligation to conduct themselves in a manner which is beyond reproach...' It concluded that Edith Cresson, a former French Prime Minister, had failed to meet that standard but that this finding was in itself an adequate penalty. No further sanction was imposed. In *Dalli v Commission* (2015), a Maltese Commissioner challenged unsuccessfully the premature termination of his term of office amid allegations that he had been involved in soliciting bribes.

The European Parliament has no legal powers to force individual Commissioners to resign, but it may require the Commission as a body to resign by passing a motion of censure on its activities. For this to happen, a very high threshold is set: a two-thirds majority of the votes cast representing a majority of its members (Article 234 TFEU). Censure motions have occasionally been tabled, but none has ever been passed. In November 2014, a motion introduced against the Juncker Commission in the wake of the LuxLeaks revelations was heavily defeated. The Parliament later set up a special committee to investigate the matter, but was hindered by lack of cooperation from multinational corporations and even some Member States.

The threat of a motion of censure was, however, exploited very effectively by the Parliament to force the resignation in March 1999 of the Commission led by Jacques Santer (and which included Edith Cresson). The trigger was a highly critical report by a Committee of Independent Experts set up on the initiative of the European Parliament to investigate allegations of fraud, mismanagement, and nepotism in the Commission. The Santer Commission had by that stage survived one motion of censure. The Committee's report made it inevitable that a new motion would be tabled and that the Commission would not survive it.

The European Parliament's standing did not rise as much as might have been anticipated following the Santer episode. One reason is that, where all the members of the Commission resign, they remain in office and continue to deal with current business until they are replaced (Articles 234 and 246 TFEU). This has practical advantages, but to the public it may look as if things are carrying on as usual. The new Commission, under the presidency of Romano Prodi, a former Italian Prime Minister, was not formally appointed until September 1999.

One of the Commission's most important prerogatives is the right to initiate the law-making process. Its importance is emphasized by Article 17(2) TEU, which provides:

> Union legislative acts may only be adopted on the basis of a Commission proposal, except where the Treaties provide otherwise. Other acts shall be adopted on the basis of a Commission proposal where the Treaties so provide.

This right of initiative enables the Commission to decide in many areas of EU competence where and when binding acts are needed and to dictate the terms of the debate.

Where the Council acts on a proposal from the Commission, it may normally amend it only by acting unanimously. The Commission, however, may amend a proposal at any time as long as the Council has not acted (Article 293(2) TFEU). Moreover, where the Commission considers that an amendment under consideration would undermine the capacity of a proposal to achieve its objectives, it may withdraw the proposal completely provided the Council has yet to act. The Commission must have due regard to the concerns underlying the proposed amendment and give reasons for its decision to withdraw, which may be challenged in the CJEU (*Council v Commission* (2015)). In its work programme for 2016, the Commission announced its intention to withdraw a number of proposals which it no longer considered relevant or timely.

The Commission is required to 'carry out broad consultations with parties concerned in order to ensure that the Union's actions are coherent and transparent' (Article 11(3) TEU). The European Parliament and the Council (though oddly not the European Council) may ask the Commission to submit proposals they consider desirable but the Commission is not obliged to comply, though it must give reasons if it decides not to do so (Articles 225 and 241 TFEU respectively). In addition, under the so-called citizens' initiative, not less than one million citizens from at least seven Member States may invite the Commission to submit a proposal where they consider that the EU needs to act in order to implement the Treaties (Article 11(4) TEU). The Commission is again free to decide whether or not to act, though it must give reasons for its decision.

Chapter 4
How secondary EU law
is made

The EU has a number of law-making procedures. They have
evolved greatly over the years, but some features have endured.
The procedures seek to reconcile swirling national, institutional,
and political rivalries. Like all legislation, the measures they
generate represent compromises but they have on the whole been
remarkably successful in achieving their objectives. However,
some say the EU makes too much law and question the democratic
legitimacy of its law-making procedures.

The ordinary legislative procedure

The most significant of the procedures available is the ordinary
legislative procedure (OLP), which applies in many important
areas of EU competence. Article 18 TFEU, for example, provides:
'The European Parliament and the Council, acting in accordance
with the ordinary legislative procedure, may adopt rules designed
to prohibit [discrimination on grounds of nationality].' Other
areas where the OLP applies are the rights of EU citizens to move
and reside freely within the Member States (Article 21(2) TFEU),
the free movement of workers (Article 46 TFEU), and freedom
of establishment (Article 50(1) TFEU).

The OLP normally starts with the submission by the Commission
to the European Parliament and the Council of a proposal for a

regulation, directive, or decision. There then begins an elaborate quadrille between the Parliament and the Council, with the Commission cast in the role of matchmaker. If successful, the procedure culminates in the joint adoption by the Parliament and the Council of a 'legislative act'.

Although potentially a difficult and lengthy process, the OLP may be cut short if agreement can be reached early. The search for common ground takes place in informal negotiations between representatives of the Parliament, the Council, and the Commission known as trilogues. If agreement is reached, it must then be formally approved by each institution. In practice, most legislation adopted under the OLP is agreed through the use of trilogues. However, they attract criticism because they take place behind closed doors and make it more difficult for national parliaments to scrutinize the passage of legislation. The European Ombudsman has called for the process to be made more transparent.

QMV in the Council applies at nearly every stage of the OLP. Occasionally, however, the Treaty inserts into the OLP additional safeguards for dissenting Member States known as 'emergency brakes'. These involve the suspension of the OLP and referral of the matter to the European Council.

The emergency brake procedure applies under Article 48 TFEU, which concerns the adoption of social security measures necessary to provide freedom of movement for workers. In principle, such measures are adopted under the OLP. However, where a Member State declares that a proposal 'would affect important aspects of its social security system... or would affect the financial balance of that system', it may invoke the emergency brake. The European Council then has four months to act. It may refer the proposal back to the Council, in which case the OLP resumes. Alternatively, it may take no action or ask the Commission to submit a new proposal. In either case, the original proposal then lapses.

The procedure operates slightly differently under Articles 82(3) and 83(3) TFEU, which deal with judicial cooperation in criminal matters under the AFSJ. They authorize the adoption of directives in accordance with the OLP. Should a Member State consider that a draft directive 'would affect fundamental aspects of its criminal justice system', it may invoke the emergency brake. If the European Council reaches a consensus within four months, it refers the draft back to the Council and the OLP resumes. If there is disagreement but at least nine Member States wish to proceed with the draft, they may do so by invoking the provisions on enhanced cooperation without having to satisfy the procedural requirements normally applicable in such cases.

Before Lisbon, action in these areas required the unanimous support of the Council. The emergency brake procedure was intended to mollify Member States uncomfortable with the transition to QMV entailed by use of the OLP.

Enhanced cooperation

The growth in the remit of the EU and in the number of its Member States has led to increasing disagreement about the speed and direction of the integration process. At the same time, there is a general view that it is preferable where possible to pursue further integration within the EU framework rather than resorting to forms of intergovernmental cooperation outside that framework.

As a result of these pressures, some important initiatives have not extended to all Member States. The most striking are EMU and the AFSJ. Another example is the Schengen Agreements, which originated outside the EU framework but were subsequently brought within it. In all three areas, some Member States have opt-outs contained in primary law.

The Treaties also provide an exceptional mechanism for enabling some Member States to proceed with a measure among themselves where there is insufficient agreement for it to be adopted in the usual way. Introduced at Amsterdam, enhanced cooperation allows at least nine Member States to make use of the EU's institutions to exercise any of its non-exclusive competences where progress has become blocked, typically because the legal basis of the proposed act requires the Council to act unanimously.

Member States wishing to trigger enhanced cooperation must send a request to the Commission, which may then submit a proposal to the Council. After obtaining the consent of the European Parliament, the Council may grant authorization to proceed. Where enhanced cooperation within the framework of the CFSP is concerned, the request goes to the Council, which decides after consulting the High Representative and the Commission. The Parliament is merely informed of the request.

Enhanced cooperation is subject to various substantive and procedural conditions designed to safeguard the integrity of the EU and the position of the Member States. Such cooperation must 'aim to further the objectives of the Union, protect its interests and reinforce its integration process' and be 'open at any time to all Member States' (Article 20(1) TEU). The Commission and participating Member States must 'promote participation by as many Member States as possible' (Article 328(1) TFEU). Enhanced cooperation must not 'undermine the internal market or economic, social and territorial cohesion', nor may it constitute a barrier to trade between Member States or distort competition (Article 326 TFEU). It must respect 'the competences, rights and obligations' of non-participating Member States, which in turn must not 'impede its implementation' (Article 327 TFEU).

The Council and the Commission are required to cooperate in ensuring 'the consistency of activities undertaken in the context of enhanced cooperation and the consistency of such activities with the policies of the Union...' (Article 334 TFEU). The decision of the Council authorizing enhanced cooperation may only be adopted 'as a last resort, when it has established that the objectives of such cooperation cannot be attained within a reasonable period by the Union as a whole...' (Article 20(2) TEU).

All Member States participate in the Council's deliberations, but only those wishing to sign up to enhanced cooperation take part in the vote, the rules for which are adapted to take account of the reduced number of Member States (Article 330 TFEU). States taking part may even agree to some relaxation of the voting rules laid down in the legal basis of the act (Article 333 TFEU). Only States taking part are bound by the act adopted, which does not have to be accepted by States seeking membership of the EU (Article 20(4) TEU).

Enhanced cooperation was first employed in 2010, when fourteen Member States were authorized to establish such cooperation in the context of the law applicable to divorce and legal separation. An earlier Commission proposal on the matter, for which the Treaty required unanimity in the Council, had been opposed by Sweden.

In *Spain and Italy v Council* (2013), a Council decision authorizing enhanced cooperation was challenged before the CJEU for the first time. The decision involved the creation of a unitary patent providing uniform protection throughout the EU. It had proved impossible to reach agreement on the applicable language arrangements, a matter for which the TFEU required unanimity in the Council. Twenty-five Member States therefore requested enhanced cooperation. The CJEU found that the conditions laid down in the Treaties had been met and dismissed the challenge.

Enhanced cooperation has so far been relatively little used. Its potential to add complexity and undermine the uniform application of EU law is self-evident. It raises the prospect that a caucus of Member States (such as members of the eurozone) might become dominant, with enough weight to form a qualified majority and using enhanced cooperation when the Treaties require unanimity. This could marginalize excluded Member States and weaken their commitment to the EU.

Special legislative procedures

The Treaty also provides for regulations, directives, and decisions to be introduced by special legislative procedure (SLP). This involves the adoption of the measure by either the Parliament or the Council but with the participation of one or the other in the procedure, as the case may be.

An example is Article 19 TFEU. This provides that '...the Council, acting unanimously in accordance with a special legislative procedure and after obtaining the consent of the European Parliament, may take appropriate action to combat discrimination' on certain specified grounds. Here the measure cannot be adopted if the Parliament objects, but it is not involved in elaborating the measure as it would be if the OLP applied. Article 19 TFEU may be contrasted with Article 21(3) TFEU, one of the provisions on citizenship of the Union. This provides: '...the Council, acting in accordance with a special legislative procedure, may adopt measures concerning social security or social protection. The Council shall act unanimously after consulting the European Parliament.' Here the Council merely has to consult the Parliament. If it fails to do so, any measure it goes on to adopt will be invalid (*Roquette Frères v Council* (1980)). However, the Council is not bound by the Parliament's view, so the Parliament cannot prevent the adoption of a measure with which it disagrees.

Some SLPs add an additional requirement that the measure adopted must be approved by the Member States following their own constitutional requirements. This means that the measure falls if it is rejected by a single Member State. An example is Article 25 TFEU, which permits the Council, 'acting unanimously in accordance with a special legislative procedure and after obtaining the consent of the European Parliament', to adopt provisions strengthening or adding to the rights of EU citizens. Such provisions enter into force only after they have been approved by the Member States in accordance with their respective constitutional requirements. The use of this procedure reflects the political importance of the issues at stake, issues which might otherwise have necessitated amendments to the Treaties.

Legislative acts

Measures adopted under the OLP or an SLP are defined by the TFEU as 'legislative acts' (see Article 289(3) TFEU). That term should therefore be confined to acts adopted under one of those procedures. This matters for several reasons. First, Article 15 TEU requires the Council to meet in public 'when considering and voting on a draft legislative act'. Secondly, draft legislative acts are subject to enhanced scrutiny by national parliaments. Thirdly, an act's legislative status affects the extent to which its validity may be challenged in the CJEU. Finally, a legislative act 'may delegate to the Commission the power to adopt non-legislative acts of general application to supplement or amend certain non-essential elements of the legislative act' (Article 290(1) TFEU). The essential elements have to be reserved for the legislative act itself, which must lay down explicitly the conditions to which the delegation is subject.

Some legally binding measures may also be adopted under the TFEU by non-legislative procedure. For example, certain measures connected with the common agricultural and fisheries policies can be adopted by the Council on a proposal from the Commission (Article 43(3) TFEU). Some agreements between management and labour may be implemented by Council decision on a proposal from the Commission. The European Parliament is merely informed (Article 155(2) TFEU). The procedures applicable in particular contexts seem to have been determined on largely pragmatic grounds. It is difficult to discern any underlying principle that might explain in every case why one procedure was preferred to another. Where a legally binding measure has to be implemented under uniform conditions, implementing powers must be granted to the Commission or exceptionally the Council (Article 291(2) TFEU). Mechanisms to enable Member States to supervise the way the Commission exercises these powers are laid down by regulation.

The choice of legal act

The legal basis under which the institutions are acting will sometimes specify the use of a particular type of act. Alternatively it may permit the institutions to choose between different acts. Where the act to be adopted is not specified, Article 296 TFEU says that 'the institutions shall select it on a case-by-case basis, in compliance with the applicable procedures and with the principle of proportionality'. The nature of the act used has no bearing on whether or not it is legislative in character. This is determined solely by whether it was adopted by legislative procedure. All acts are required to 'state the reasons on which they are based' and 'refer to any proposals, initiatives, recommendations, requests or opinions required by the Treaties' (Article 296 TFEU).

The field of competition law illustrates how different acts may be deployed. Article 87 EEC gave the Council a legal basis for the adoption of *regulations or directives* to give effect to the principles set out in Articles 85 and 86 EEC, which laid down the competition rules applicable to businesses. Since those rules were unfamiliar to most of the then Member States, the Council decided to introduce a centralized system for their application. This meant that a *regulation* rather than a *directive* was appropriate.

In 1962 Regulation 17 was adopted giving the Commission extensive powers to apply and enforce the Treaty competition rules. These included powers to address *decisions* to businesses requiring them to supply information, submit to investigations by Commission officials at their premises, and terminate infringements, and to impose fines on infringing firms of up to 10 per cent of their turnover in the preceding business year.

In May 2004, a new Council *regulation* to give effect to the Treaty competition rules entered into force modernizing the regime laid down in Regulation 17. Based on Article 83 EC, Regulation 1/2003 devolved greater responsibility to the national competition authorities and courts and gave the Commission enhanced powers to tackle major cartels and abuses of market power.

A provision which did not specify the type of instrument to be used was Article 235 EEC. Sometimes known as the flexibility clause, this provided:

> If action by the Community should prove necessary to attain, in the course of the operation of the common market, one of the objectives of the Community and this Treaty has not provided the necessary powers, the Council shall, acting unanimously on a proposal from the Commission and after consulting the European Parliament, take the appropriate measures.

This broad residuary power risked undermining the principle of conferral unless close attention were paid to the need for the proposed action if the Community's objectives were to be met. The Court's initial failure to scrutinize that issue sufficiently strictly meant that Article 235 came to be seen as a way of making what were effectively small changes to the Treaty: if all the national governments were in agreement, what possible objection could there be?

In 1996, the CJEU tightened up its approach to Article 235, making it clear that it could not be used as the basis for 'provisions whose effect would, in substance, be to amend the Treaty…' (Opinion 2/94). There was later some support for removing the flexibility clause from the Treaties, but it found its way into the

TFEU as Article 352. That provision is more limited in scope than Article 235 EEC and its use is subject to extra procedural safeguards. Its significance is reduced because the EU has over the years been given many more specific powers than those originally conferred on the EEC. This makes it more difficult to maintain that, in areas where action by the EU is necessary, 'the Treaties have not provided the necessary powers'. Article 352 still does not require the use of any particular type of instrument.

The decision-making process involving the adoption of one of the instruments listed in Article 288 TFEU after full participation by the Commission, the European Parliament, and the Council, with qualified majority voting by the Member States and judicial scrutiny by the CJEU, is known as the 'Community method'. It limits the influence of individual Member States and is the gold standard to which the EU in principle aspires.

Sometimes, however, Member States worry about the threat posed to national sovereignty by the Community method. It is for this reason that decision-making under the CFSP remains predominantly intergovernmental: the European Council and the Council normally act unanimously; the adoption of legislative acts is excluded; and the jurisdiction of the CJEU is severely curtailed (Article 24(1) TEU). The implications of the Community method also explain the gradual way it has been introduced in the AFSJ and the opt-outs enjoyed by some Member States in that field.

Does Brussels interfere too much?

There has been a big increase in the EU's legal output over the last thirty years or so. This is partly due to decisions taken by the Member States to increase the EU's powers. However, concerns have mounted about the resultant regulatory burden on Member States, businesses, and individuals. In April 2016, Commission President Juncker acknowledged that 'we were wrong in over-regulating and interfering too much in the daily lives of our citizens'.

An important part of the Commission's response to such concerns is its Regulatory Fitness and Performance Programme (REFIT). This is intended to eliminate unnecessary regulatory costs and ensure that EU legislation is fit for purpose. Its political importance was underlined when Juncker gave his first Vice-President, former Dutch Minister of Foreign Affairs Frans Timmermans, the task of ensuring 'better regulation'. In his State of the Union address to the European Parliament on 14 September 2016, Juncker said that the Commission had withdrawn 100 proposals in its first two years in office, presented 80 per cent fewer initiatives than over the previous five years, and launched a review of all existing legislation.

A more formal safeguard against interference by the EU in areas that could have been left to the Member States is the principle of subsidiarity, which must be satisfied before the EU may act wherever it does not have exclusive competence. Given general application at Maastricht, this principle is now laid down in Article 5(3) TEU, which says: '…the Union shall act only if and in so far as the objectives of the proposed action cannot be sufficiently achieved by the Member States…but can rather, by reason of the scale or effects of the proposed action, be better achieved at Union level'.

The TEU links the principle of subsidiarity with that of proportionality. In the present context, the latter principle means that EU action must not 'exceed what is necessary to achieve the objectives of the Treaties' (Article 5(4) TEU). While subsidiarity is about *whether* the EU should exercise a competence conferred on it, proportionality is about *how far it should go* in doing so.

Some maintained that the issue of subsidiarity was essentially a political one to be resolved during the process leading to the adoption of an act. Others thought it was suitable in the last resort for application by the CJEU. In the event, neither the politicians nor the judges showed any enthusiasm for applying the principle.

In the 'Working Time Directive' case, for example (see Box 4), the CJEU simply said that, once the Council had decided that common minimum requirements on the health and safety of workers were needed, Community-wide action was inevitable. Juncker acknowledged in April 2016 that 'we were wrong insufficiently to respect subsidiarity'.

At Lisbon, an attempt was made to reinforce both subsidiarity and proportionality by enlisting the help of the national parliaments. Draft legislative acts must now be forwarded to the national parliaments along with a detailed explanation of why both principles are satisfied. National parliaments have eight weeks to object if they consider that a draft legislative act does not comply with the principle of subsidiarity (though not proportionality). Where the number of objections reaches a certain threshold, the draft has to be reviewed by its author, who may decide to maintain, amend, or withdraw it. It must give reasons for its decision. (This is sometimes called the 'yellow card' procedure.) In certain cases, the objections of the national parliaments and the justification for the measure have to be taken into account by the legislator. (This is sometimes called the 'orange card' procedure.) The CJEU has jurisdiction to hear challenges notified by Member States on behalf of their national parliaments to legislative acts on the ground that they infringe the principle of subsidiarity. (This is sometimes called the 'red card' procedure.)

Though national parliaments do not always confine their objections to subsidiarity, these arrangements seem to have had some effect in reinforcing that principle and encouraging national parliaments to take a closer interest in EU affairs. The explanation given of why subsidiarity is satisfied, any objections raised by national parliaments, and the response of the measure's author might encourage the CJEU to exercise its review powers more robustly in the event of a challenge. The House of Lords EU Committee has recommended that the procedure should be enlarged to allow national parliaments to object to draft measures on grounds of proportionality and choice of legal basis. It rejected the suggestion that a 'yellow card' should automatically have the effect of blocking draft legislation, but suggested that where this does not occur the draft should be substantially amended.

Does the EU suffer from a 'democratic deficit'?

Article 2 TEU says that 'democracy' is one of the values on which the EU is founded. To what extent do the policies and rules adopted by the EU themselves enjoy democratic legitimacy? Article 10 TEU attempts to answer that question. It points out that citizens are 'directly represented at Union level in the European Parliament'. It emphasizes that the politicians who represent the Member States in the European Council and the Council 'are themselves democratically accountable either to their national Parliaments, or to their citizens'. These features clearly inject an element of democracy into the EU, but is it enough?

The fundamental problem is that the EU does not have a democratically elected government. This means that there is never an opportunity for voters 'to throw the scoundrels out', to borrow a phrase coined by Joseph Weiler of New York University and the EUI, Florence. As Weiler has pointed out, there have been 'some spectacular political failures of European governance', but these have not led 'to any measure of political accountability, of someone paying a political price for their failure, as would be the case in national politics'. Moreover, the influence of national governments in the EU's decision-making process and the difficulties national parliaments sometimes experience in scrutinizing them tend to enhance the power of national executives at the expense of national legislatures.

Attempts have been made to address the latter difficulty in two ways. First, EU consultation documents and draft legislative acts must now be forwarded to national parliaments in good time to make it easier for them to hold their governments to account.

Secondly, as I have explained, national parliaments now have a formal role in policing the application of the principles of subsidiarity and (to a lesser extent) proportionality. However, it has proved difficult to find a way of giving them more direct influence over the content of EU measures.

Despite successive increases in its powers, the European Parliament has not solved these problems. Its failure to connect with the European electorate is reflected in the decline in turnout in every set of direct elections since the first in 1979. As the Bundesverfassungsgericht (the German Federal Constitutional Court) pointed out in its *Lisbon* decision (2009), the Parliament is not 'a representative body of a sovereign European people'. Weiler concludes that 'the two most primordial norms of democracy, the principle of accountability and the principle of representation, are compromised in the very structure and process of the Union'.

We may see this as a fundamental flaw in the whole venture. Alternatively, we may say that the EU is as democratic as it is possible to make such a complex entity and more democratic than other international organizations. Some might add that deficiencies in the process by which rules are made (so-called 'input legitimacy') may be compensated by the success of the rules themselves in enhancing welfare (so-called 'output legitimacy'). If that argument was ever persuasive, its credibility was seriously undermined by the eurozone crisis. I discuss this in Chapter 9.

Chapter 5
On the origin of treaties

The EU Treaties are international agreements signed by sovereign States and ratified by each one following their own constitutional requirements. They enter into force once this process is complete. To that extent, the EU is a creation of international law (sometimes called the law of nations). However, in the seminal case of *Van Gend en Loos v Nederlandse Administratie der Belastingen* (1963), the CJEU declared that '...the [EU] constitutes a new legal order of international law for the benefit of which the states have limited their sovereign rights...'. It later described the Treaties as the EU's 'basic constitutional charter' and 'an independent source of law' (Opinion 2/13 (2014)).

Some therefore argue that the EU has cast off its origins in international law and now occupies a class of its own. EU law is increasingly treated by scholars as distinct from international law and is starting to resemble a national system in its scope and complexity. The CJEU has spoken of the 'autonomy enjoyed by EU law in relation to the laws of the Member States and in relation to international law' but at the same time emphasized that the EU is 'precluded by its very nature from being considered a State' (Opinion 2/13 (2014)). On the contrary, it is an international organization to which the Member States have granted certain powers to attain common objectives (Article 1 TEU).

Amending the Treaties

The Treaties are, not surprisingly, more difficult to amend than secondary EU law. Now set out in Article 48 TEU, the amendment procedure originally involved the submission by a Member State or the Commission of a proposal to the Council, which was required to consult the European Parliament and, where appropriate, the Commission. If the Council was in favour, a conference of national governments (known as an intergovernmental conference or IGC) would be convened to decide what, if any, changes should be made. These had to be agreed by all national governments. They would be incorporated in a new treaty, which would enter into force only after being ratified by each Member State according to its own constitutional requirements. At Maastricht, this procedure was altered slightly to provide for consultation of the European Central Bank (ECB) where institutional changes in the monetary area were being contemplated. Otherwise, the procedure remained unchanged until the Treaty of Lisbon.

This bald description of the treaty amendment procedure conveys nothing of the drama which has sometimes accompanied national ratification due to the increasing use of referendums in Member States. This was done for the first time in connection with the SEA, which was approved by referendum in Denmark and Ireland in 1986 and 1987 respectively. The problems began with the more ambitious Treaty of Maastricht, which was rejected by referendum in Denmark in 1992. Later the same year, that Treaty was only narrowly approved in a referendum held in France. This was a watershed moment for the EU, confronting it for the first time with clear evidence of disquiet among the general public at the way in which the integration process was unfolding.

Technically the outcome of the 1992 referendum in Denmark might have sounded the death knell for the Maastricht Treaty. It could only enter into force if ratified by all the Member States and

Denmark was now unable to do so. However, the other Member States embarked on an attempt to respond to the apparent concerns of the Danish people in a way which did not require the painstakingly crafted Treaty to be reopened. At a summit meeting in Edinburgh in December 1992, Denmark was given a number of assurances. These paved the way for a second referendum in May 1993 when a significant majority of the Danish electorate approved the Treaty, allowing it to enter into force the following November.

The Maastricht Treaty was therefore saved, but an unfortunate precedent was set. Critics started to say that, when the EU did not like the outcome of a national referendum, it simply asked people to carry on voting until they got the right answer. That impression was reinforced when the Irish people were required to vote twice in referendums on both the Nice Treaty (in 2001 and 2002) and the Lisbon Treaty (in 2008 and 2009).

Only one amending Treaty has been killed off by negative votes in national referendums: the Treaty Establishing a Constitution for Europe (Constitutional Treaty) agreed by the Member States in October 2004. The Constitutional Treaty's 448 articles represented an ambitious attempt to replace the existing Treaties with a new treaty having overt constitutional pretensions and equipping the EU with some of the trappings of a State. It was based on a draft prepared by the so-called Convention on the Future of Europe, which included representatives of the European Parliament, the national parliaments, the Member States, and the then candidate countries.

Referendums on the Constitutional Treaty held in France and the Netherlands in May and June 2005 respectively produced decisive 'no' votes. The Constitutional Treaty was pronounced dead in 2007, when the Member States announced that they were abandoning the 'constitutional concept' and that the reforms necessary would be introduced in the classic way by means of amendments to the existing Treaties. The result was the Lisbon Treaty.

This episode compounded the unfortunate impression being created about the EU's responsiveness to direct expressions of the popular will. Why were the French and the Dutch not asked to vote again like the Danes and the Irish? Could it be that founding Member States (especially if very large) were considered more significant than smaller latecomers? There again, the Lisbon Treaty contained many provisions that had featured in the Constitutional Treaty. Had the exercise simply been a ruse to avoid asking the French and the Dutch to vote again, or to avoid the referendum on the Constitutional Treaty that the government of Tony Blair had announced in 2004 would be held in the UK?

One of the features of the Constitutional Treaty that was incorporated into the TEU at Lisbon was a new process for changing the Treaties. This now comprises an ordinary procedure and two simplified procedures. The ordinary procedure makes express provision for the involvement of a convention to consider the proposed changes and make a recommendation to an IGC. Where the European Parliament agrees, the European Council may decide not to convene a convention if the extent of the proposed amendments is too limited to justify that step. The Treaty now clarifies that amendments may either increase or reduce the EU's powers.

Under the first of the simplified procedures, the European Council may amend Part Three of the TFEU, which is concerned with the policies of the EU, by adopting a unanimous decision after consulting the European Parliament and the Commission (and sometimes the ECB). To enter into force, the decision must be approved by the Member States following their own constitutional requirements. It must not increase the EU's powers.

Under the second of the simplified procedures, the European Council (acting unanimously and with the consent of the European Parliament) may adopt a decision simplifying the way the Council of Ministers has to act in certain areas. Any such decision has to be notified to the national parliaments and can only be adopted if none of them objects.

These procedures are designed to respond to a number of concerns. Notwithstanding the failure of the Constitutional Treaty, conventions are seen as more transparent than the often secretive IGCs. They also allow a wider range of stakeholders to take part. It is, however, recognized that the so-called 'convention method' can make the process unduly cumbersome. Two particular cases are identified where the convention method does not apply. Both contain protections for the Member States. An attempt has also been made to counter a perception that Treaty changes inevitably lead to an increase in the EU's powers.

While there was a flurry of amending Treaties between the SEA and the Treaty of Lisbon, the 2004 and 2007 enlargements seem to have dulled the EU's appetite for further changes. The larger the EU gets, the more likely it becomes that a revising treaty will be blocked or delayed by a negative referendum result in one of the Member States. There is now a strong preference for working within the existing framework wherever possible.

Where this cannot be achieved, recourse is sometimes made to international treaties adopted outside the framework of the EU. One example is the Schengen Agreements. Another is the Treaty on Stability, Coordination, and Governance (or 'Fiscal Compact') signed by twenty-five of the then Member States in 2012 as part of the EU's response to the eurozone crisis. An attempt to incorporate the terms of the Fiscal Compact in the EU Treaties had been blocked by the UK and the Czech Republic. As a matter of EU law, international treaties concluded by Member States outside the EU framework must comply with the EU Treaties. This was made clear in *Pringle v Ireland* (2012), where the CJEU upheld the legality of the European Stability Mechanism (ESM) Treaty, another international agreement concluded by eurozone Member States in response to the financial crisis.

Joining the EU

The Treaties are also amended when a new Member State joins the EU. Enlargement of the EU was for a long time seen as a fundamental element of the integration process and the Treaties have always contained a procedure for allowing additional States to join (or 'accede'). After the fall of the Berlin Wall in 1989, and with the prospect of the accession of several central and eastern European countries (CEECs), the EU's capacity to absorb new members was questioned: how might enlargement affect the EU's ability to function effectively and achieve its policy goals?

The right to apply for membership is open to '[a]ny European State which respects the values referred to in Article 2 [TEU: see Box 5] and is committed to promoting them...'. The term 'European' has become increasingly problematic as membership of the EU has grown. Allan Tatham of Péter Pázmány Catholic University, Budapest, observes that it 'combines geographical, historical and cultural elements and its essence is regarded differently by each succeeding generation'. In 1987, the Council rejected an application from Morocco, doubtless on the basis that it was not a European State.

Box 5 Article 2 TEU

The Union is founded on the values of respect for human dignity, freedom, democracy, equality, the rule of law and respect for human rights, including the rights of persons belonging to minorities. These values are common to the Member States in a society in which pluralism, non-discrimination, tolerance, justice, solidarity and equality between women and men prevail.

An aspiring member (see Box 6) must submit an application to the Council. The European Parliament and the national parliaments are notified. After consulting the Commission, the Council authorizes the opening of negotiations. This step can only be taken if the Council is unanimous and it has the consent of the European Parliament. The process can therefore be blocked at this stage by a single Member State or the European Parliament.

Throughout this part of the procedure, the Treaty requires account to be taken of the conditions of eligibility laid down by the European Council. This evokes the so-called Copenhagen criteria originally agreed by the European Council in 1993 in preparation for the future accession of the CEECs. Those criteria require candidate countries to show respect for democracy; the rule of law and human rights; the existence of a functioning market economy; and the capacity to assume the obligations of membership.

Membership negotiations take place between the Member States and the candidate country in an IGC, with the Commission playing an important role behind the scenes. The candidate country will be expected to meet benchmarks for the adoption of existing EU law (known as the *acquis communautaire*) and the capacity to apply it

Box 6 Prospective Member States

EU CANDIDATE COUNTRIES

Country	Date of application
Turkey	1987
Former Yugoslav Republic of Macedonia	2004
Montenegro	2008
Albania	2009
Serbia	2009

properly. Once the negotiations have been successfully concluded, the detailed arrangements for the candidate country's entry into the EU are embodied in an accession treaty signed by the candidate country and all the existing Member States.

The accession treaty must then be ratified by each of the signatories in line with their own constitutional requirements. This sometimes involves national referendums. Norway has twice signed accession treaties and twice (in 1972 and 1994) seen them rejected in national referendums. It remains outside the EU. In France, a referendum was held in 1972 on the first enlargement of the EU. A referendum must in principle now be held before France may ratify accession treaties: only exceptionally may ratification be authorized by parliamentary vote. Once the process of ratification is complete, accession takes place on the date specified in the treaty, which forms part of the EU's primary law.

Christophe Hillion of the Universities of Leiden and Stockholm has observed that the authors of the EEC Treaty 'crafted a classic state-centred accession procedure inspired by the canons of international institutional law…'. Other than the Council (which consists of representatives of the Member States), the only institution originally involved was the Commission, whose role appeared to be confined to delivering an opinion on applications. The requirement that the European Parliament must consent before negotiations could be opened was introduced by the Single European Act, while the reference to the European Council was added by the Lisbon Treaty. These changes, together with the influential role in practice played by the Commission, have made the process less State centred and are consistent with the view of an EU in the process of shedding its international law origins.

Leaving the EU

Until the Lisbon Treaty, there was no formal procedure for Member States to leave the EU. Indeed, whether they even had the right to do so was disputed. Those who saw the EU as a creation of international law took the view that the EU Treaties could ultimately be repudiated by a contracting State like other international treaties. Others saw withdrawal as incompatible with the very nature of the EU, in particular the commitment to 'ever closer union' and the unlimited duration of the Treaties.

The issue was never really put to the test. The Treaties ceased to apply to Algeria following its independence from France in 1962 and in 1985 Greenland withdrew after having been granted home rule by Denmark. These were rather special cases, but they supported the view that there was no obstacle of principle to withdrawal. Indeed, when the UK held a referendum on its continued membership in 1975, it seemed to be accepted on all sides that a no vote would have led to its withdrawal.

The Lisbon Treaty added to the TEU an express provision for withdrawal, Article 50 TEU, which had first appeared in the Constitutional Treaty. A Member State which decides to withdraw must notify the European Council. The EU must then negotiate with the State concerned and conclude an agreement with it 'setting out the arrangements for its withdrawal, taking account of its future relationship with the Union'. No IGC is convened. If the agreement secures the consent of the European Parliament, it is concluded on behalf of the EU by the Council, which acts by qualified majority. As an act of secondary law the withdrawal agreement cannot modify the Treaties. The necessary changes (e.g. to the list of Member States in Article 52(1) TEU, the provisions on the territorial scope of the Treaties in Article 355 TFEU, and any special protocols covering the withdrawing State) could presumably be made under the ordinary revision procedure without convening a convention.

The Treaties cease to apply to the State concerned from the entry into force of the withdrawal agreement or, failing that, two years after the notification of its intention to withdraw. This period can be extended if all Member States (including the withdrawing

State) agree. The withdrawing State does not participate in discussions of the European Council or the Council or in decisions concerning it. If having left it later asks to rejoin, it must follow the normal accession process described earlier in this chapter.

The inclusion of this procedure in the Treaties underlines the voluntary nature of EU membership. Hillion observes that it reflects a wish to submit withdrawal 'to the canons of the EU legal order, instead of leaving it to the vicissitudes of international law'. As he points out, the international law rules on the repudiation of treaties are now excluded under the general principle that a specific rule prevails over a more general one. The process is intended to be quicker and easier than accession because of the disruption liable to be caused by the continued participation of a Member State that has announced its wish to withdraw. The withdrawal agreement cannot be blocked by a single Member State and it does not require national ratification. Even if blocked by the European Parliament, withdrawal cannot be postponed for more than two years without the agreement of the withdrawing State.

The possibility that the withdrawal process might soon have to be used arose following the election in the UK in May 2015 of a Conservative Government committed to holding a referendum on the UK's continued membership. To lay the ground for the referendum, the UK reached a legally binding agreement with the other Member States on 19 February 2016. Its central element was a decision of the HoSG 'concerning a new settlement for the United Kingdom within the European Union'. That decision addressed four themes of special concern to the UK: economic governance; competitiveness; sovereignty; and social benefits and free movement. It was to enter into force when the UK informed the Council that it had decided to remain a member of the EU.

Shortly after the settlement was agreed, it was announced that the referendum would take place on 23 June 2016, when voters

5. Campaigning in the 2016 UK referendum. (a) The Vote Leave Campaign. (b) The In Campaign Limited.

would be asked: 'Should the United Kingdom remain a member of the European Union or leave the European Union?' (see Figure 5). Following a long and divisive campaign, 51.9 per cent voted to leave the EU while 48.1 per cent voted to remain. The turnout was 72.2 per cent.

The result of the referendum, which was only advisory, proved contentious. Concerns about the veracity of some of the claims made during the campaign led to calls for a second referendum to be held. Scotland having voted overwhelmingly in favour of remaining in the EU, the Scottish Government immediately raised the possibility of a second independence referendum.

The morning after the referendum, the then Prime Minister David Cameron announced that he would resign when a successor had been chosen and leave to that person the responsibility for invoking Article 50. Following an unexpectedly short leadership contest, Theresa May became Prime Minister on 13 July 2016. One of her first acts was to establish a Department for Exiting the European Union to oversee negotiations and establish the UK's future relationship with the EU. On 2 October 2016, May announced that Article 50 would be invoked by the end of March 2017. However, on 24 January 2017 the Government's control over the process was weakened when the UK Supreme Court ruled that it lacked the power to invoke Article 50 without parliamentary enabling legislation (*R (Miller) v Secretary of State* (2017)).

Once the withdrawal process commences, the immediate task will be to reach agreement on two issues. The first is how to disentangle the UK from the rest of the EU. For example, what should be done about EU nationals resident in the UK and UK nationals resident in the EU, EU bodies based in the UK, UK staff working in EU institutions? The second is the framework for the UK's future relations with the EU. This will need to be fleshed out subsequently.

On withdrawal, legislation repealing the European Communities Act 1972, which gives legal effect in the UK to the obligations of EU membership, will take effect. It will convert EU rules into domestic rules. Decisions will then be taken on whether or not they should be retained. The outcome of this process may depend on the extent to which the UK secures continued access to the internal market. Withdrawal will mean that the UK is no longer covered by the many trade deals concluded by the EU, so it will need to strike new ones with third countries. All this could occupy Parliament, the Government, and the Civil Service for many years.

General principles of law and fundamental rights

The EU's primary law is not confined to the Treaties. It also includes the general principles of law, a body of unwritten principles used by the CJEU to fill gaps and resolve ambiguities in the Treaties and measures adopted by the institutions. Such principles have been described by the CJEU as having 'constitutional status' (*Audiolux* (2009); *NCC Construction Danmark* (2009)).

In formulating general principles, the CJEU draws inspiration from two main sources: the constitutional traditions of the Member States and international treaties they have signed. This helps to ensure that EU law remains grounded in the basic legal values of the Member States and the international community. When the CJEU recognizes a general principle of law, however, it is adapted to the particular context of the EU and develops independently of its domestic or international antecedents.

General principles bind the EU's institutions. They may affect the validity and interpretation of secondary EU law or form the basis of an action for damages against the EU. General principles also bind the Member States when they act within the scope of EU law and can be invoked by litigants in the national courts. In addition, they may be invoked in cases where the compliance of a Member State with its Treaty obligations is challenged in the CJEU.

The category of general principles is an open one, but certain such principles have become well established. An example is legal certainty, which essentially means that the rules applicable in particular circumstances should be reasonably clear and their effect predictable. Other examples are proportionality and equality or non-discrimination. In *Mangold* (2005), the CJEU controversially held that the principle of non-discrimination on grounds of age constituted a general principle of Union law.

I'd like to say a little bit more about a final example: the principle of respect for fundamental rights. Although the EEC Treaty did not originally say anything about fundamental rights, the CJEU developed that principle in a line of cases starting with *Stauder v Ulm* (1969). It suffered from the disadvantage of lacking public visibility and not articulating the precise rights it protected, so in 1999 the Member States set up a convention—the forerunner of the Convention on the Future of Europe—with the task of drawing up a Charter of Fundamental Rights for the EU. The Charter was 'solemnly proclaimed' by the European Parliament, the Council, and the Commission in 2000. Not initially legally binding, the Treaty of Lisbon gave it 'the same legal value as the Treaties'. It therefore now belongs to the EU's primary law.

According to Article 51(1) of the Charter, it is addressed mainly to the EU institutions. The CJEU has said that respect for the rights it contains is 'a condition of the lawfulness of EU acts, so that measures incompatible with those rights are not acceptable in the EU' (Opinion 2/13 (2014)). The Charter binds EU institutions even when they act outside the legal framework of the EU. The EU may therefore be liable in damages to a private party whose Charter rights are infringed by an institution in the context of an initiative like the ESM Treaty (*Ledra Advertising* (2016)).

Article 51(1) says that the Charter binds the Member States only 'when they are implementing Union law'. The CJEU has interpreted this clause to mean when they are acting within the ambit of EU law (*Åkerberg Fransson* (2013)). In such cases, national courts must apply the Charter in preference to national guarantees of fundamental rights, even where the latter offer the claimant greater protection (*Melloni* (2013)). In *Pringle*

(2012), the CJEU held that the signatory States were not implementing EU law when they adopted the ESM Treaty. Unlike the institutions, they were not therefore constrained by the Charter in that context.

The CJEU is the ultimate arbiter of the effect of the Charter. This means that the institutions of the EU are not currently subject to specialized external review for compliance with fundamental rights. The Treaty of Lisbon therefore made provision for the EU to accede to the European Convention on Human Rights (ECHR). This was originally drawn up in 1950 under the aegis of the Council of Europe, an international organization independent of the EU but to which all its Member States belong. It is under the ECHR that the European Court of Human Rights (ECtHR) in Strasbourg was established.

Article 6(3) TEU says that the fundamental rights guaranteed by the ECHR 'constitute general principles of the Union's law'. However, as the EU has not yet acceded to the ECHR, it 'does not constitute a legal instrument which has been formally incorporated into the legal order of the EU' (Opinion 2/13 (2014)). By virtue of Article 216(2) TFEU, accession would make the ECHR an integral part of EU law, 'binding upon the institutions of the Union and on its Member States' (Opinion 2/13 (2014)). In particular, it would bring the EU within the jurisdiction of the ECtHR.

However, accession would not make the ECHR part of the EU's primary law, so the former would be subject to the latter. This is because accession would be effected by an international agreement concluded by the Council under the TFEU. As an act of an institution, the accession agreement would be subject to review by the CJEU.

A draft accession agreement was agreed in April 2013, but in December 2014 the CJEU declared it incompatible with EU law

(Opinion 2/13 (2014)). The CJEU was concerned about the effect of the agreement on the autonomy of EU law and on its own position, particularly its right to rule on the compatibility of an EU measure with the ECHR before the ECtHR did so. The draft will therefore have to be amended before it can be agreed by the EU and the Council of Europe. To enter into force, it would then have to be ratified by all EU Member States and by contracting parties to the ECHR who are not members of the EU. This process is strewn with pitfalls and is likely to take some time to complete.

Chapter 6
EU law in the national courts

Direct effect and primacy

In September 1960, a company called Van Gend en Loos imported into the Netherlands from Germany a quantity of a substance called urea formaldehyde. The Netherlands charged the company import duty of 8 per cent. The company objected. It pointed out that the duty payable on such substances when the EEC Treaty entered into force in 1958 was only 3 per cent. Article 12 of that Treaty said that Member States should not increase the duties they had been applying in their trade with each other. The dispute reached the Tariefcommissie in Amsterdam, an administrative court with jurisdiction in the Netherlands over customs matters. What the Tariefcommissie did next led to a decision of the CJEU which, although little noticed at the time, would later be seen as perhaps the most important it has ever given.

The problem confronting the Tariefcommissie was that the EEC Treaty did not explain how conflicts in national courts between provisions of the Treaty and national law should be resolved. The domestic effect of international treaties normally depended on the national law of the contracting States. However, in a common market the law must apply uniformly throughout the countries belonging to it. This could not be achieved if some of them allowed its rules to be enforced in their national courts while others did not.

In *Van Gend en Loos v Nederlandse Administratie der Belastingen* (1963), the Tariefcommissie therefore decided to ask the CJEU whether a trader could rely in circumstances such as these on Article 12 EEC to challenge the increase in import duty. In reply, the CJEU observed that the Treaty did more than merely create mutual obligations between the contracting states, the classic international law position. On the contrary, EU law was also intended to confer on individuals 'rights which become part of their legal heritage'. Article 12, the CJEU noted, contained 'a clear and unconditional prohibition...'. Its implementation was not dependent on further action by the national legislatures. These features helped make it 'ideally adapted to produce direct effects in the legal relationship between Member States and their subjects'. The fact that the article was addressed to the Member States did not in the CJEU's view imply that their nationals could not rely on it, for that would be to deprive them of direct legal protection for their rights. Moreover, allowing them to do so would create an army of private enforcers, thereby strengthening a power the Treaty grants the Commission to take legal action against delinquent Member States. The CJEU therefore ruled that Article 12 produced direct effect, creating individual rights which national courts had to protect.

It might have been argued that the case was limited to disputes between private claimants and the State or a public authority (known as *vertical* disputes) and to negative provisions of the Treaty like Article 12. However, the CJEU later made it clear that Treaty provisions might also produce direct effect in proceedings between private parties (known as *horizontal* disputes) and even if positive in character. The crucial issue was whether the provision concerned was clear enough to be applied by a national court.

The CJEU's ruling in *Van Gend* did not explain how the Tariefcommissie was to resolve the conflict between Article 12 and the inconsistent provision of national law invoked by the respondent authority. The Tariefcommissie had not put that question to the CJEU because it was settled by Netherlands law, which said that directly effective provisions of international agreements enjoyed primacy over national law.

The question of primacy was raised directly in *Costa v ENEL* (1964), a reference by an Italian judge concerning the compatibility with the EEC Treaty of a 1962 Italian law. International law was not generally understood to require national courts to enforce treaty provisions which conflicted with national law. However, the uniform application of EU law could not have been ensured if a directly effective treaty provision could be overridden by a contrary rule of national law. The CJEU therefore declared:

> The transfer by the States from their domestic legal system to the [EU] legal system of the rights and obligations arising under the Treaty carries with it a permanent limitation of their sovereign rights, against which a subsequent unilateral act incompatible with the concept of the [EU] cannot prevail...

The CJEU's reasoning implied that EU law would enjoy primacy regardless of the constitutional status under national law of the conflicting domestic rule or the date on which that rule was adopted, whether before or after the entry into force of the Treaty. That implication was confirmed in *Internationale Handelsgesellschaft* (1970), where it was made clear that both primary and secondary rules of EU law enjoyed primacy over national rules whenever adopted and even if they had constitutional status.

Very occasionally, overriding interests such as legal certainty have led the CJEU to limit the effect of these doctrines. In *Defrenne II* (1976), for example, it held that a Treaty article on equal pay for men and women had direct effect but could only in limited circumstances be invoked retrospectively. This was to cushion the effect of the ruling on employers, who had been led to believe that legislation was necessary to give effect to the equal pay principle laid down in the Treaty. In *Inter-Environnement Wallonie v*

Région Wallonne (2012), the CJEU permitted a national court to preserve temporarily a national measure which did not comply fully with EU rules on environmental protection. The CJEU considered that allowing the measure to remain in force for a short period would be less harmful to the environment than quashing it immediately before it could be replaced.

The late Hjalte Rasmussen of the University of Copenhagen cited *Costa v ENEL* as a case 'in which the Court probably pushed its gap-filling activities beyond the proper scope of judicial involvement in society's law and policy making'. However, just because the Treaty did not expressly give EU law primacy over national law did not necessarily mean that this was not intended. Once the question was raised by a national court, the CJEU had no choice but to craft an answer which was consistent with the spirit of the Treaty. It is significant that *Van Gend* and *Costa* attracted no immediate political response.

Following the Luxembourg Compromise of 1966 and the EU's failure to complete the common market by the end of the transitional period, the CJEU used the doctrine of direct effect to ensure that the integration process did not lose momentum. Two years before *Defrenne II*, the CJEU held that the Treaty rules on establishment (*Reyners v Belgium* (1974)) and services (*Van Binsbergen v Bedrijfsvereniging Metaalnijverheid* (1974)) produced direct effect from the end of the transitional period even though the Council had failed to adopt the implementing directives envisaged by the Treaty. It was in the 1970s that the CJEU's influence and prestige reached its peak and its place in the founding myth of the EU as both architect and saviour of the integration process was consolidated.

The direct effect of EU acts

In the 1980s the institutions and the Member States began to play a more active role in the functioning of the EU and the case law on the direct effect of EU acts gathered pace. By and large, regulations and decisions had not caused the CJEU much difficulty. Since the former were described by the Treaty as 'directly applicable', it was widely assumed that litigants could rely on them in the national courts where they were sufficiently clear, an assumption endorsed by the CJEU in *Variola* (1973). Decisions may be enforced in the national courts against those who are bound by them (*Grad v Finanzamt Traunstein* (1970)). This means either their addressees, where they are specified, or anyone falling within their scope (Article 288 TFEU).

By contrast, directives would spawn a labyrinthine body of case law whose twists and turns can test even the most assiduous reader. The essential question is what happens if a Member State fails to implement a directive properly? Can an individual who would have benefited rely on it directly before the national courts? In short, can directives produce direct effect?

Many assumed initially that, because directives needed national implementation, this was not possible. However, in the 1970s the CJEU established that directives could be directly effective in the *vertical* sense. The case law was summarized in *Becker* (1982). There the CJEU said that, in vertical cases where the deadline for implementation had passed, a directive could be invoked by individuals in national courts provided its content was unconditional and sufficiently precise. A Member State could not in such cases rely in its defence on its own unlawful conduct in failing to implement the directive.

Rasmussen was highly critical of this case law, arguing that it was not supported by the text of the Treaty and declaring: 'To many a European lawyer this is revolting judicial behaviour.' That view was reflected in the decisions of some national courts. A notable example is that of the French Conseil d'État in the *Cohn-Bendit* case (1978), where in flagrant disregard of the case law of the CJEU an individual was prevented from relying on a directive to challenge a national measure. National judicial opposition may well have influenced the CJEU when it confronted the question whether directives could not only confer rights on individuals but also require them to do things, in other words, produce *horizontal* direct effect.

That question was finally tackled in *Marshall v Southampton and South-West Hampshire Area Health Authority* (1986), a sex discrimination case, where the CJEU pointed out that the Treaty only made a directive binding on 'each Member State to which it is addressed'. It followed that a directive 'may not of itself impose obligations on an individual and that a provision of a directive may not be relied upon as such against such a person'. Stephen Weatherill of the University of Oxford observed: 'In return for such clarification and such restraint [the CJEU] hoped to gain from the national courts an acceptance of that more restricted notion of direct effect—against the state alone. The tactic seems largely to have worked.'

Be that as it may, the CJEU's reasoning in *Marshall* was not entirely convincing. Its emphasis on the wording of the Treaty seemed inconsistent with its approach in *Van Gend* and *Defrenne II*, both of which also concerned Treaty provisions addressed to the Member States. In *Defrenne II*, the CJEU stated that 'the fact that certain provisions of the Treaty are formally addressed to the Member States' did not stop them from conferring rights on individuals. Moreover, the importance attached by the CJEU to the notion of 'State' meant that a claimant's rights might depend exclusively on the status of the defendant, an apparently arbitrary criterion. Because the remit of the State might vary from country to country, it risked undermining the effectiveness of directives, which are intended to lay down common rules.

In *Faccini Dori v Recreb* (1994), a consumer protection case, the CJEU reconsidered the position but refused to depart from *Marshall*. However, although the consequences for individuals and the uniform application of EU law were potentially serious, the CJEU found ways of mitigating the effect of those cases. Three are worth mentioning here.

First, the notion of State was widely construed by the Court. In *Marshall* itself, the respondent was a regional health authority, not part of central government. The CJEU nonetheless concluded that it was a public authority and that the directive in question could be invoked against it. In *Foster* (1990), another sex discrimination case, the CJEU held that directives could be invoked against any body 'which has been made responsible, pursuant to a measure adopted by the State, for providing a public service under the control of the State' and has been given special powers beyond those normally enjoyed by individuals.

Secondly, when national courts apply domestic law, they are bound if possible to interpret it in the light of the wording and the purpose of any overlapping directive so that the directive's aims are met. This obligation is not confined to national provisions adopted specifically to give effect to a directive: it extends to all provisions of national law whenever they were adopted.

This principle of consistent interpretation is subject to certain qualifications (*Angelidaki* (2009)). It does not require national law to be given a meaning that is contrary to its clear terms. It cannot create criminal liability where it would not otherwise exist or increase the penalty for an existing offence. It applies in only a diluted form before the deadline for giving effect to a directive has passed.

The principle of consistent interpretation is less intrusive than direct effect because the outcome is determined by national law. It is also more flexible, because the national court has some discretion in determining how much leeway it enjoys in interpreting its national law. However, these features make the principle less effective than direct effect in protecting the rights of individuals under EU law. Moreover, the principle weakens legal certainty by creating doubt about the effect of national law.

In *Mangold*, the CJEU found a third way of escaping from the shackles of *Marshall*. *Mangold* concerned the interpretation of Directive 2000/78, which deals with combating discrimination in employment on a variety of grounds, including age and sexual orientation. It was adopted by the Council under Article 13 EC, now Article 19(1) TFEU. In proceedings before a German court brought against a lawyer by one of his employees who claimed he had been discriminated against because of his age, the CJEU was asked for guidance on its effect.

The directive might have seemed irrelevant, for the dispute was a horizontal one and the deadline for implementing the directive had not expired at the material time. However, the CJEU declared that the source of the principle of equal treatment in the field of employment was not the directive itself but 'various international instruments' and 'the constitutional traditions common to the Member States'. The principle of non-discrimination on grounds of age therefore constituted a general principle of EU law. The national court had 'to guarantee the full effectiveness of the general principle of non-discrimination in respect of age, setting aside any provision of national law which may conflict with [EU] law'.

In *Kücükdeveci* (2010), the CJEU made it clear that the prohibition of age discrimination did not have to be applied in cases falling outside the scope of EU law. Nonetheless, *Mangold* proved highly controversial. It implied that, when a directive was found to enshrine a general principle of EU law, individuals would be able to rely directly on that principle notwithstanding *Marshall* in horizontal cases which fell within the scope of EU law. The application of *Mangold* by the German courts was the subject of a complaint (ultimately unsuccessful) to the Bundesverfassungsgericht (*Honeywell* (2010)).

In defence of *Mangold*, we might point out that the principle of non-discrimination is well established and is enshrined in Article 21 of the now binding Charter of Fundamental Rights. We may think it right that it should keep pace with contemporary attitudes. On the other hand, general principles of law had not previously been considered directly effective in and of themselves. The principle of non-discrimination is not an absolute one but may be subject to exclusions and justifications, the precise scope of which must be spelled out in implementing measures such as Directive 2000/78. Moreover, the approach of the CJEU seems inconsistent with Article 19 TFEU, which entrusts the Council with the task of deciding how to combat discrimination.

The CJEU followed *Mangold* in a case involving discrimination on the ground of sexual orientation (*Römer* (2011)). However, it seems reluctant to apply the same approach to other principles. *Dominguez v CICOA* (2012) involved the right to paid annual leave. Such a right is enshrined in the Working Time Directive and it was described by the CJEU in that case as 'a particularly important principle of EU social law'. Even though it features in Article 31(2) of the Charter of Fundamental Rights, the ruling in *Dominguez* makes it clear that it cannot be applied directly in horizontal situations. So *Mangold* may apply only to discrimination on the grounds referred to in Article 19 TFEU. The fact that the Treaty specifically singles out those grounds might perhaps be said to underline their particular importance.

Claiming damages where a Member State breaches EU law

In *Francovich* (1991), the CJEU added the finishing touch to the picture it began to paint in the 1960s. An employee protection case, the CJEU there held 'that the Member States are obliged to make good loss and damage caused to individuals by breaches of [EU] law for which they can be held responsible'. That obligation was said to be both 'inherent in the system of the Treaty' and included among the 'appropriate measures' which Member States were required by Article 4(3) TEU to take to ensure performance of their obligations.

Claims for damages against a Member State were to be brought in the national courts, which would have to make available the standard range of remedies to ensure that the rights of claimants were protected effectively. Claimants would have to show that the rule of EU law alleged to have been infringed was intended to confer rights on individuals; that the infringement was sufficiently serious, in the sense that the defendant had manifestly and gravely disregarded the limits on its discretion under EU law; and that there was a direct causal link between the infringement and the damage sustained (*Brasserie du Pêcheur and Factortame* (1996)). State liability may exceptionally result from an infringement of EU law by a top national court (*Köbler v Austria* (2003)).

What is the relationship between State liability and direct effect? In *Brasserie du Pêcheur and Factortame*, the CJEU said that, where a Member State infringed a directly effective provision of EU law, the right to reparation was 'the necessary corollary' of its direct effect, because otherwise 'the full effectiveness of [EU] law would be impaired'. However, *Francovich*, which involved a breach of a directive that was found not to be directly effective, had shown that direct effect was not essential to a finding of State liability. Indeed, State liability might be the only remedy available to a claimant in such cases. Thus, in *Faccini Dori* the CJEU specifically drew the referring court's attention to the obligation of a Member State to make good damage caused to individuals through its failure to transpose a directive.

Sionaidh Douglas-Scott of Queen Mary, University of London, has argued that *Francovich* left the CJEU 'open to the charge of judicial lawmaking and the undermining of the rule of law'. The German Government put forward a similar argument in *Brasserie du Pêcheur and Factortame*. The CJEU responded robustly.

It noted that, since the Treaty did not deal expressly with the consequences of a breach of EU law by a Member State, it was for the CJEU to rule on the matter. It pointed out that, under the second paragraph of Article 340 TFEU, the liability of the EU itself for damage it had caused was based on the general principles common to the laws of the Member States. That provision reflected, it said, 'the general principle familiar to the legal systems of the Member States that an unlawful act or omission gives rise to an obligation to make good the damage caused' and the obligation of public authorities 'to make good damage caused in the performance of their duties'. The CJEU added: 'in many national legal systems the essentials of the legal rules governing State liability have been developed by the courts.'

In practice the principle of State liability has not developed as vigorously as might have been expected. The CJEU has upheld the liability of Member States in clear cases of failure to comply with their obligations or where the denial of liability might completely nullify the applicant's rights. However, fears that Member States would be found liable in damages for inadvertent failures to implement directives have proved unfounded. The CJEU has been willing to make allowances where EU rules are ambiguous. It has also taken a strict approach to causation. The *Köbler* case suggests that it is only in the most extreme cases that a State will incur liability for the actions of a top court.

The underlying rationale for State liability applies equally to infringements of EU law by private parties. There seems to be a general right to recover damages in such circumstances (*Muñoz and Superior Fruiticola* (2002)), but it is in the field of competition law that the right is most developed. A party to a contract that infringes the Treaty may recover damages from the other party for loss suffered as a result of the infringement (*Courage v Crehan* (2001)), as may third parties (*Manfredi* (2006)). The CJEU has even held that, where a cartel contrary to the Treaty causes an increase in prices, anyone who has paid those higher prices may recover damages from members of the cartel even in the absence of any contractual link with them (*Kone AG and Others v ÖBB-Infrastruktur AG* (2014)).

Legal and procedural hurdles in the Member States meant that such claims for a long time remained few in number. In November 2014, the Council therefore adopted a directive designed to make it easier for victims of infringements of EU competition law to claim damages in the national courts from those responsible.

The reaction of national courts

The CJEU said in Opinion 2/13 that the basic principles of EU law, including primacy and direct effect, were

> based on the fundamental premiss that each Member State shares
> with all the other Member States, and recognises that they share
> with it, a set of common values on which the EU is founded . . .
> That premiss implies and justifies the existence of mutual trust
> between the Member States that those values will be recognised
> and, therefore, that the law of the EU that implements them will
> be respected.

The national courts now routinely apply the doctrines of direct effect as well as primacy insofar as it affects national legislation and subordinate national laws. However, top national courts have baulked at the idea that EU law should enjoy primacy over national rules having constitutional status. This is because, from the national viewpoint, the effect of EU law in the national systems is determined not by EU law but by national law, of which top national courts are the ultimate guardians. They may say that national law does not permit the absolute primacy of EU law to be recognized or does not permit the government to transfer powers to an organization which asserts absolute primacy. That view is clearly inconsistent with the case law of the CJEU.

The standard-bearer for national judicial resistance to the full implications of primacy is the Bundesverfassungsgericht, which has asserted (but not yet exercised) a constitutional power of its own to police the protection of fundamental rights in the EU (*Internationale Handelsgesellschaft mbH v Einfuhr- und Vorratsstelle für Getreide und Futtermittel* (1974)), ensure respect by the EU institutions for the limits of their powers (*Brunner v European Union Treaty* (1993)), and uphold what it calls Germany's 'constitutional identity' (*Re Ratification of the Treaty of Lisbon* (2009)).

Approaches similar to that of the Bundesverfassungsgericht have been taken in other Member States, including Italy, Denmark, and the UK. In the 'Slovak Pensions' case (2012), the Czech Constitutional Court said a decision of the CJEU was outside its powers on the basis that it exceeded those transferred to the EU under the Czech Constitution. The stance of the Bundesverfassungsgericht has had an effect on the attitude of the CJEU, leading it to find a way of securing protection for fundamental rights in the EU and to take more seriously its responsibility for policing the limits of the EU's powers.

The possibility of conflict arose in *Gauweiler v Deutscher Bundestag* (2015), where the CJEU took a different view from that of the Bundesverfassungsgericht of the EU's powers in the field of EMU. Ultimately, the Bundesverfassungsgericht accepted the CJEU's ruling. What might the consequences have been if there had been a direct clash?

The formal position in EU law is clear. As the CJEU pointed out in Opinion 1/09 (2011), it would have been open to anyone incurring a loss as a result to claim damages from Germany in its own courts. Moreover, the Commission would have been entitled to bring proceedings against Germany before the CJEU. These might in theory have led to the imposition on Germany of a financial penalty. However, the late Sir Neil MacCormick of the

University of Edinburgh advised national courts to avoid conflict through circumspection and political as much as legal judgment. In practice, that advice has been followed by most national courts, including perhaps the Bundesverfassungsgericht in *Gauweiler*.

The Lisbon Treaty introduced a provision with the potential to soften the edges of the primacy doctrine in cases where important national principles are at stake. Article 4(2) TEU requires the EU to respect the 'national identities' of the Member States insofar as they are inherent in their fundamental political and constitutional structures. It will be the CJEU which ultimately decides what that means.

Chapter 7
The Court of Justice of the European Union

I'd now like to take a closer look at another of the EU's institutions, the CJEU. The basic duty of the CJEU is to ensure that 'the law is observed' in the interpretation and application of the Treaties (Article 19(1) TEU). That duty is reinforced by the inclusion of the rule of law among the values on which the EU is founded (see Article 2 TEU). Located in Luxembourg, the CJEU mustn't be confused with the European Court of Human Rights, which is based in Strasbourg, France, and is not an institution of the EU.

Most of the cases brought before the CJEU fall into one of two categories. *Direct actions* start and finish in Luxembourg. By contrast, *references for preliminary rulings* originate in a national court which finds itself in need of guidance on the effect of EU law before giving judgment. It therefore asks the CJEU for a ruling which it then applies to the facts of the case.

The CJEU has three component parts, the most important of which are the Court of Justice and the General Court.

The Court of Justice

The Court of Justice consists of one judge from each Member State (Article 19(2) TEU). It may sit as a chamber of three or five judges, a Grand Chamber of 15 judges, or a full Court comprising all the judges (see Figure 6). Normally the larger the formation, the more difficult or important the case is thought to be. A party may not object to the composition of the Court of Justice on the basis of the presence or absence of a judge of a particular nationality. In 2015, the Court of Justice received 713 new cases and decided 616. It had a backlog of 884 cases.

The Court of Justice is assisted by eleven Advocates General, who enjoy the same status as judges. They have counterparts in some of the Member States of continental Europe. The Treaties do not say anything about the nationality of the Advocates General. However, it is the practice of the Member States that there should always be an Advocate General from the six largest Member States (France, Germany, Italy, Poland, Spain, and for the time being the UK), the remaining posts rotating among the other Member States.

6. A hearing before a five-judge chamber of the Court of Justice.

The role of an Advocate General is to deliver an opinion to the Court of Justice on the case under consideration. This is done after any hearing has taken place and before the Court of Justice begins its deliberations. The contribution made by Advocates General to the comprehensibility and even coherence of the case law of the Court of Justice is widely recognized. The Court of Justice delivers a single collegiate judgment whose main purpose is to declare what the law is. The reasons it gives for its conclusions are often terse and sometimes the result of compromise between the judges involved. Dissenting judgments, where a judge expresses his or her disagreement with the view of the majority, are not permitted. By contrast, an Advocate General's Opinion is the work of a single author and often provides a more thorough analysis of the issues raised by a case than the judgment.

Until the Treaty of Nice, an Advocate General's Opinion was required in each case brought before the Court of Justice. However, the preparation of an Opinion causes delay and it came to be accepted that in simple cases Opinions were unnecessary. The default position remains that an Advocate General will assist the Court in all cases. However, the Court of Justice may now decide to do without an Opinion where it thinks that a case 'raises no new point of law' (Statute, Article 20). In 2015, around 43 per cent of judgments were given without an Opinion.

The General Court

The General Court (formerly the Court of First Instance) was set up in 1988 to relieve pressure on the Court of Justice resulting from its growing workload and to create a specialized fact-finding tribunal. In 2015 the General Court received 831 new cases and decided 987. It had a backlog of 1,267 cases. These figures show that its capacity to manage its own workload is becoming problematic.

The General Court deals at first instance with all direct actions brought by private applicants. It also handles direct actions brought by Member States against: (a) certain acts of the Council; (b) nearly all acts of the Commission; and (c) all acts of the ECB. The General Court has no jurisdiction at present to give preliminary rulings, though this may change in the future.

Decisions of the General Court on questions of fact are final, but on points of law can be taken on appeal to the Court of Justice. The appeal rate in 2015 was 27 per cent. The success rate is relatively low: of the 134 appeals decided by the Court of Justice in 2015, only 25 were wholly or partly upheld. These figures are a measure of how successful the General Court has been.

The General Court must include 'at least one judge per Member State' (Article 19(2) TEU). The precise number is laid down in Article 48 of the Statute of the CJEU, which may be amended by the European Parliament and the Council acting in accordance with the OLP on a request from the Court of Justice or a proposal from the Commission (Article 281 TFEU). Following a request from the Court of Justice, the Council agreed in December 2015 to increase the number of judges from one to two per Member State over a period ending on 1 September 2019. The aim was to help the General Court cope with its workload and reduce the EU's potential liability in damages if the General Court failed to give judgments within a reasonable period of time, as required by Article 47 of the EU's Charter of Fundamental Rights.

Most cases brought before the General Court are dealt with by a three- or five-judge chamber. The General Court may also be constituted as a single judge or sit as a Grand Chamber or full court, but this hardly ever happens. There are no full-time Advocates General in the General Court, but judges may be asked to perform the role of Advocate General in difficult or complex cases. This is rarely done.

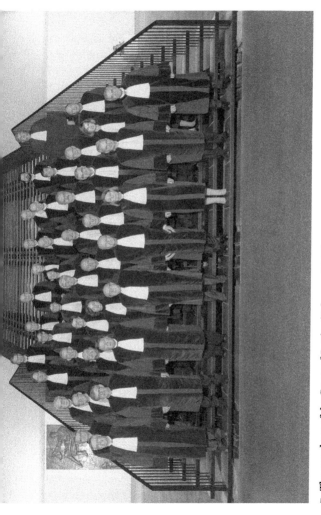

7. The members of the Court of Justice (February 2016).

Members of the CJEU

Judges and Advocates General of the Court of Justice must be 'persons whose independence is beyond doubt'. They must either 'possess the qualifications required for appointment to the highest judicial offices in their respective countries' or be 'jurisconsults of recognised competence' (Article 253 TFEU). In practice the members of the Court of Justice have come from a range of professional backgrounds, from the national judiciaries and the Bar to the civil service and universities (see Figure 7). British critics have sometimes objected to members without judicial experience, but the House of Lords EU Committee has cautioned against 'trying to impose on other Member States a particularly British view of the best background for senior judicial office'.

Members of the General Court must also be 'persons whose independence is beyond doubt'. They must 'possess the ability required for appointment to high judicial office' (Article 254 TFEU).

Members of both the Court of Justice and the General Court serve for renewable terms of six years (with the exception of Advocates General from Member States which do not have such a post permanently and whose terms are not in practice renewed). They are appointed by agreement among the governments of the Member States. In theory, this means that a national nominee could be blocked by other Member States but they hardly ever seem to have done so. This led to concerns that some individuals were being appointed for reasons other than their legal aptitude.

Article 255 TFEU therefore introduced a requirement that a panel should be consulted by national governments before appointments to the Court of Justice or the General Court were made. The panel comprises seven individuals 'chosen from among former members of the Court of Justice and the General Court, members of national supreme courts and lawyers of recognised competence, one of whom shall be proposed by the European Parliament'. Its members are appointed by the Council for terms of four years, renewable once. It deliberates in private but must give reasons for its opinions. Although not formally binding, they are in practice followed.

Judicial approach

The approach of the CJEU has been heavily influenced by the civil law tradition of the six original Member States, although the influence of the common law began to be felt with the accession in 1973 of the UK and Ireland. The civil law and the common law are two of the world's great legal 'families'. To oversimplify, the characteristic feature of the civil law is its reliance on codified abstract rules; that of the common law, the importance attached to decided cases.

While the activities of the General Court are of interest mainly to specialists, the Court of Justice is more controversial. This is because of the role it has played in crafting many of the fundamental principles of EU law and its approach to the interpretation of the Treaties. This has given it a reputation in some quarters as an activist or political court. One critic asserted:

> The Court of Justice has indulged in 'creative jurisprudence' on many occasions. The Treaty texts and directives agreed between the Member States may at any time be given by the Court a meaning and impetus that may not have been contemplated by the negotiators.

The problem with this sort of criticism is that activism is often in the eye of the beholder: if you disapprove of the outcome of a case from a policy perspective, you are more likely to consider it activist. Moreover, those who accuse the Court of Justice of activism often fail to give sufficient weight to 'the characteristic features of [EU] law and the particular difficulties to which its interpretation gives rise' (*CILFIT v Ministry of Health* (1982)). Prominent among these are the gaps and ambiguities in the Treaties, especially in their original form, and their multilingual nature. There are now official versions of the TEU, the TFEU, and EU acts in twenty-four languages, each of which has the same status. The Court of Justice therefore had little choice but to interpret them in the light, not just of their wording, but also of their objectives and legal context.

Another objection sometimes voiced by critics is that the Court of Justice does not adequately engage with the arguments of the parties or show how its decisions fit with previous case law. The way the Court of Justice handles its own previous decisions is partly attributable to its civil law origins. While the Court of Justice endeavours to respect its established case law, it does not treat it as binding or feel compelled to reconcile new decisions with previous judgments in the manner of a common law court. Be that as it may, its reasoning is sometimes inadequate to explain changes in the direction of its case law. An example is the *Mangold* case, where the Court of Justice offered only meagre justification for its radical conclusion that there was a general principle prohibiting discrimination on the grounds of age that individuals could invoke in the national courts.

Chapter 8
Enforcing EU law

What powers does the CJEU have to make sure the law is observed? In this chapter, I'm going to look at three of the most important. One involves Member States which have failed to do what the Treaties require of them. One involves challenging the legality of things the EU has done. One involves helping national courts to apply EU law correctly.

Infringement proceedings

Under Article 258 TFEU, the Commission may bring proceedings before the Court of Justice against any Member State which breaches its obligations under EU law. Potential breaches by Member States come to the attention of the Commission in a variety of ways. These include its own monitoring of the application of EU law and complaints from individuals, businesses, NGOs, and other stakeholders.

The Commission has discretion to decide whether or not to launch proceedings. It cannot be forced to do so (*SDDDA v Commission* (1996)). Certain cases are given priority. These include those involving the implementation of directives; those affecting growth in the internal market; and those involving the implementation of EU legislation on asylum.

The Commission may be handling many complaints and infringement files at any one time. It aims to decide within twelve months of registering a complaint whether to close the case or launch formal proceedings. Most complaints are not pursued. Member States try hard to settle out of court those that are, so many fall by the wayside as the procedure advances.

Of the cases that proceed to judgment, most are won by the Commission. In 2015, an infringement was declared in twenty-six cases, while five applications were dismissed. In that year the Member States with the highest number of infringement actions brought against them were Germany, Greece, and Portugal (four each). Overall Italy has most often been the subject of such actions, having been the defendant on 642 occasions by the end of 2015.

Where there are lots of infringements in a particular area of EU activity, this may indicate that there are implementation problems that need to be addressed. An understanding of the challenges faced by Member States in implementing and applying EU law is also important at the policy development stage, where it can help in assessing whether a proposal is feasible.

The essential question in infringement proceedings is whether, objectively speaking, the situation in the defendant State is consistent with EU law. This may lead the State concerned to challenge the Commission's understanding of what EU law in fact requires and whether its national law implements it correctly. It may also argue that the Commission did not conduct the procedure properly. However, except where there has been an unpredictable and overwhelming catastrophe making compliance impossible (a situation known as *force majeure*), the Court of Justice will not be interested in the explanation for any breach established by the Commission.

Where the Commission wins the case, the Member State concerned must do what is necessary to comply with the judgment. If it fails to act promptly, the Court of Justice may impose financial sanctions on it (Article 260(2) TFEU). These may take the form of a lump sum or a penalty payment which increases the longer the failure continues. The sanctions procedure requires the Commission to go back to the Court of Justice, specifying the amount of the sanction it considers appropriate. The amount set will reflect the seriousness of the infringement, its duration, the need to deter further infringements, and the Member State's capacity to pay. The Court of Justice often reduces the amount suggested by the Commission.

In *Commission v France* (2005), the Court of Justice said that a lump sum and a penalty payment might both be imposed in serious cases, particularly where the breach had continued for a long time and was likely to persist. That case concerned a failure by France to comply with EU rules on the conservation of fish stocks. France was required to pay: (a) a penalty payment of €57,761,250 for each period of six months from delivery of the second judgment during which the breach persisted; and (b) a lump sum penalty of €20,000,000.

The Commission's annual report for 2015 on the application of EU law concluded that 'ensuring timely and correct application of EU legislation in the Member States remains a serious challenge'. The sanctions available play a useful if modest role in encouraging Member States to comply with their obligations. The report observed: 'At the end of 2015, seven infringement procedures were still open after a Court ruling under Article 260(2).' This suggests that the sanctions imposed are sometimes not heavy enough to ensure speedy compliance.

Since Lisbon, a simplified procedure for imposing sanctions has applied in cases where a Member State fails to give effect to 'a directive adopted under a legislative procedure' (Article 260(3) TFEU). This gives Member States a stronger incentive to transpose legislative directives in a timely manner. In 2015, 543 cases of late transposition were opened by the Commission and it made five applications to the Court of Justice under Article 260(3). Four such cases remained unresolved at the end of that year.

A more radical procedure is laid down in Article 7 TEU. This provides for the Treaty rights of a Member State to be suspended by the Council where it is found by the European Council to have committed 'a serious and persistent breach...of the values referred to in Article 2 [TEU]...' The procedure to be followed is a very heavy one (see Article 354 TFEU). The Member State concerned may challenge the legality of the act of the European Council or the Council in the Court of Justice, but on procedural grounds only (Article 269 TFEU). This prevents the Court of Justice from reviewing the political assessment of the alleged breach. Article 7 does not provide for the expulsion of Member States.

In January 2016, the Commission took the unprecedented step of launching a review of changes in Poland to its laws on the media and the functioning of its Constitutional Court, a move that could lead to the application of Article 7. The use of that article against certain Member States over their response to the migration crisis has also been mooted.

The action for annulment

Imagine the EU suspects you of terrorism and adopts a measure freezing your assets. Perhaps it alleges that you have broken the Treaty competition rules and imposes a hefty fine on you. What if it stops you from using a tried and tested name to describe your products and you are worried about the effect on your sales? Is there anything you can do to protect your rights?

In an organization founded on the rule of law, it would have been surprising if the answer to that question were 'no'. Article 263 TFEU accordingly provides for an action for annulment to allow the validity of EU acts to be challenged.

Annulment actions can be brought against any act adopted by legislative procedure and any act (even if not adopted by legislative procedure) of the Council, the Commission, or the ECB. Such actions may also be used to challenge acts of the European Parliament, the European Council, or 'bodies, offices or agencies of the Union' (see Box 7) provided they produce legal effects vis-à-vis third parties, that is, parties who did not play a role in the adoption of the act.

In order to succeed, the applicant must show that the measure being challenged is unlawful. The Treaty sets out four grounds on which this may be done. The grounds are based on French administrative law and cover virtually all possible forms of illegality. For example, a measure may be annulled if it contravenes the Treaty or a general principle of law or pursues an end other than that stated. It may suffer the same fate if the adopting institution lacked the authority to adopt it or did not follow the correct procedure.

Where the applicant's claim succeeds, the act concerned is declared void (Article 264 TFEU). The institution concerned

---

Box 7 Bodies, offices, or agencies of the EU

The term 'bodies, offices, or agencies' means bodies set up by legislation to implement specific EU policies. The numerous examples include:

(a) the European Union Intellectual Property Office;
(b) the European Union Agency for Fundamental Rights;
(c) the European Institute for Gender Equality;
(d) the European Environment Agency;
(e) the European Medicines Agency;
(f) the European Chemicals Agency.

must do what is necessary to comply with the judgment (Article 266 TFEU). The judgment may lead to a claim for damages against the EU under Article 340 TFEU. In principle, the judgment entitles everyone to treat the offending act as if it had never existed. To avoid a legal vacuum, however, the CJEU may preserve some of its effects until it has been replaced (Article 264 TFEU).

If anyone could bring annulment proceedings, the CJEU might be swamped and the functioning of the EU seriously disrupted. In the national systems it is common for procedures of this sort to be confined to those who can establish 'standing', in other words that they are particularly affected in some way by governmental action. EU law follows suit. Annulment proceedings may only be brought by applicants who satisfy standing rules laid down in the TFEU. An applicant who is unable to establish standing will not be permitted to ask the CJEU to examine the legality of an EU act.

Three categories of applicant are distinguished. The first two are relatively straightforward.

The Member States, the European Parliament, the Council, and the Commission are sometimes called 'privileged applicants'. They are presumed to have an interest in the legality of all EU acts and automatically have standing without having to establish any particular interest. This is so regardless of the position they adopted during the legislative procedure. The term 'Member State' for this purpose means central government and does not include the governments of regions or autonomous communities, such as Catalonia or the Basque country in Spain and Flanders or Wallonia in Belgium. These constitute non-privileged applicants, which I shall come to.

The Court of Auditors (the EU's financial watchdog), the ECB, and the Committee of the Regions (representing regional interests) are sometimes called 'semi-privileged applicants'. They can only bring proceedings for the purpose of protecting their position in the EU's decision-making processes.

That leaves so-called natural and legal persons (mainly companies and individuals, regardless of their nationality). Sometimes called 'non-privileged' or 'private' applicants, their position is more complicated. They can automatically challenge acts addressed to them. However, the standing rules they must satisfy if they want to challenge any other type of act are complex and have been interpreted strictly by the CJEU. Although they were relaxed slightly at Lisbon in cases involving non-legislative acts, they remain very demanding.

In *Inuit* (2013), a challenge to a regulation restricting trade in seal products, the applicants were found to lack standing to proceed. The CJEU acknowledged that everyone had a fundamental right to effective judicial protection of their rights, but justified its strict approach to standing on the basis that it shared responsibility for upholding that right with the Member States and their courts. It emphasized that the validity of EU acts could be reviewed by national courts through the preliminary rulings procedure.

The preliminary rulings procedure

EU law assumes that the rules it lays down will apply uniformly to all those who are subject to them. It also gives a good deal of the responsibility for applying those rules to the national courts of the Member States. This poses a potential risk. Left to their own devices, it is unlikely that courts in, say, Dublin would always apply EU law in the same way as courts in, say, Warsaw.

To guard against that risk, Article 267 TFEU enables (and sometimes obliges) national courts to refer to the Court of Justice questions of EU law that need to be decided before they can give judgment. A question may concern the interpretation or effect of a provision of EU law or the validity of an EU act.

It is hard to exaggerate the importance of this procedure. Courts can only decide issues raised by cases brought before them. The preliminary rulings procedure has brought before the Court of Justice a host of issues it might not otherwise have had a chance to consider. It has enabled it to influence directly the application of EU law in the Member States. The Court of Justice has described it as the 'keystone' of the judicial system established by the Treaties, having 'the object of securing [the] uniform interpretation of EU law..., thereby serving to ensure its consistency, its full effect and its autonomy as well as, ultimately, the particular nature of the law established by the Treaties' (Opinion 2/13 (2014)).

The ruling given by the Court of Justice in reference proceedings binds the referring court, which must apply it to the facts of the case. This means it is not the Court of Justice but the referring court which is responsible for disapplying national law if it turns out to be incompatible with EU law. Other national courts are entitled to treat the ruling of the Court of Justice as settling the issue, though they may if they wish refer the same or a related question to the Court of Justice themselves for further clarification.

At Lisbon, Article 267 was amended to require the Court of Justice to 'act with the minimum of delay' in cases involving people in custody. This is particularly important in cases covered by the AFSJ, where an urgent preliminary ruling procedure (or PPU: *procédure préjudicielle d'urgence*) may be used. Under the PPU, the procedure is simplified. To date, cases dealt with under the PPU have been resolved significantly more quickly (in an average of just under two months in 2015) than cases dealt with under the standard procedure (just over fifteen months on average in 2015).

The success of the reference procedure depends on the willingness of the national courts to make references to the Court of Justice and then to apply its rulings faithfully. Some of those rulings have encountered opposition in certain national courts. Barristers David Anderson QC and Marie Demetriou QC divide cases in which national courts have resisted rulings supplied by the Court of Justice into three categories: those where there is a conflict between EU law and values enshrined in national constitutions; those where the national court takes the view that the Court of Justice has exceeded its jurisdiction; and those where the national court has disliked the ruling given by the Court of Justice and sought to avoid applying it. By and large, however, the national courts have played their part in the procedure remarkably conscientiously. Why is this?

One reason sometimes advanced is the persuasive force of judgments delivered by a court comprising eminent lawyers from all the Member States in language to which national courts are accustomed. Pierre Pescatore, a judge at the Court of Justice from 1967 to 1985, said of its decision in *Van Gend en Loos*: 'There has rarely been a legal argumentation as well developed as this one, and presented to individuals and their judges with such elegance and persuasive power.' Another reason is the tendency of Article 267 to promote competition between national courts. It can subvert national judicial hierarchies by enabling lower courts to bypass superior courts and converse directly with the Court of Justice and to do things (like disapplying legislation) that might otherwise be outside their powers.

Of the 713 new cases brought before the Court of Justice in 2015, 436 were references for preliminary rulings. There is quite a wide variation in the number of references from each Member State. In 2015, the highest number of references came from Germany (79), followed by Italy (47). Historically, Germany is well ahead of the other Member States, with a total of 2,216 references, followed by Italy with 1,326 and the Netherlands 949, by the end of 2015.

Once allowance has been made for length of membership, the variation seems to be due partly to differences between Member

States in the volume of economic activity in areas subject to EU law. However, for references to be generated in significant numbers, there still needs to be a constituency within a Member State with an interest in attacking national rules that do not comply with EU law and the means to do so. The large number of references made by German courts is sometimes said to have increased the impact of German law and legal thinking on the development of EU law.

The relationship between the national court and the Court of Justice in reference proceedings is cooperative rather than hierarchical in nature. Both courts have distinct but complementary roles to play in finding a solution to the case that is compatible with EU law. A reference to the Court of Justice is not an appeal against the decision of the national court. The parties to the action before the referring court have the right, along with the Member States, the Commission, and sometimes other institutions and bodies, to submit observations to the Court of Justice, but technically there are no parties to the reference proceedings themselves, which take the form of a 'dialogue' between the Court of Justice and the referring court (Opinion 2/13 (2014)).

Article 267 distinguishes between top national courts (courts 'against whose decisions there is no judicial remedy under national law') and other national courts. The latter enjoy discretion in deciding whether to ask for a preliminary ruling on questions of interpretation. Instead of making a reference they may decide what EU law means for themselves. It may be best for them to do so where the answer is reasonably clear.

However, the Court of Justice is far better equipped than national courts to resolve issues of EU law. As Mr Justice Bingham acknowledged in the English case of *Commissioners of Customs and Excise v Samex ApS* (1983), the Court of Justice has 'a panoramic view of the [EU] and its institutions, a detailed knowledge of the Treaties ... and an intimate familiarity with the functioning of the [EU] market which no national judge...could hope to achieve'.

A national court cannot be deprived of its power to make a reference by a ruling of a superior court. This was underlined in *Križan* (2013), a dispute over the location of a landfill site. There a judgment of the Slovakian Supreme Court was overturned by the Slovakian Constitutional Court, which referred the case back to the Supreme Court so that it could give a fresh ruling. Under Slovakian law, the Supreme Court was bound by the ruling of the Constitutional Court, but the former was uncertain whether the position of the latter was compatible with EU law. It therefore made a reference to the Court of Justice. The Court of Justice declared that a national court was entitled to make a reference in these circumstances and would be bound by the ruling of the Court of Justice even if it meant disregarding the ruling of the higher court. *Križan* exemplifies clearly the capacity of the preliminary rulings procedure to subvert domestic legal hierarchies.

Top national courts are in principle obliged to refer to the Court of Justice questions of EU law that need to be decided before they give judgment. Failure to do so may exceptionally expose the State concerned to infringement proceedings or claims for damages by litigants deprived of their rights under EU law. In *Križan*, the Court said that the Slovakian Supreme Court was a top court for this purpose. Although its decisions could be challenged before the Constitutional Court, the circumstances in which this could be done were too limited to constitute a 'judicial remedy'. The Court of Justice thereby contrived to reinforce further the position of the more europhile of the two national courts.

In *CILFIT v Ministry of Health* (1982), the Court of Justice held that top national courts were under no obligation to refer if the point at issue had already been dealt with by the Court of Justice or the answer was obvious (a situation known as *acte clair*).

However, before the national court reaches that conclusion, a number of conditions must be met. Some take the view that those conditions are too strict, but the obligation of top national courts to refer helps to protect the rights of litigants and maintain uniformity. That view was accepted at the Nice IGC, where the Member States declined to pursue a suggestion that the Treaty should be amended to relax the obligation.

Questions of *validity* (as opposed to *interpretation*) typically arise in reference proceedings where a national measure based on an EU act is challenged in a national court on the ground that the underlying EU act is unlawful. In a departure from the strict terms of Article 267 TFEU, it was held in *Foto-Frost v Hauptzollamt Lübeck-Ost* (1987) that national courts may not declare EU acts invalid. The main reason for this is that divergence between courts in different Member States over the validity of EU acts would pose a particularly serious threat to the unity of the EU legal system.

So where a national court thinks that a challenge to an EU act might be well founded, it is obliged to refer the question of its validity to the Court of Justice. The only exception is where a national court is asked to make an interim order suspending an act to preserve the status quo pending judgment in a case. Jurisdiction to declare EU acts invalid is therefore the exclusive preserve of the CJEU. This means that top national courts cannot avoid referring questions of *validity* by reference to the *CILFIT* case: this applies only to questions of *interpretation* (*Gaston Schul Douane-Expediteur* (2005)).

The possibility that an EU act might be declared invalid in reference proceedings is a useful complement to the action for annulment. However, the emphasis the Court of Justice now places on reference proceedings to justify its strict stance on the standing rules applicable to private applicants in annulment proceedings is curious. Annulment proceedings involve a direct challenge to an act before the one court which can rule on its validity. By definition reference proceedings must go through the filter of the national court. This is likely to discourage some claimants and seems self-evidently less efficient and less effective than annulment proceedings.

Chapter 9
Coping with crises

The eurozone crisis

Even if the common market had been completed on time, it would still have been easier for a company based in Paris to do business with one based in Bordeaux than one based in Frankfurt. The reason is simple: a German company would not have used the same currency as a French one.

To solve this problem, the objective of establishing an EMU started to appear on the EU's agenda in the early 1970s and later formed part of the discussions around the completion of the internal market in the late 1980s. However, it was not until the Maastricht Treaty was signed that formal arrangements for replacing the national currencies of the Member States with a single currency, later called the euro, were made. Those arrangements fell short of those canvassed in the early 1970s in one important respect: they envisaged that aspects of economic policy would continue to be set at national rather than EU level. That fateful choice would have devastating consequences.

Article 3(4) TEU says that the EU must 'establish an economic and monetary union whose currency is the euro'. Article 119 TFEU requires the Member States and the EU to pursue a single monetary policy and exchange-rate policy with the primary objective of maintaining price stability. Three guiding principles must be respected: 'stable prices, sound public finances and monetary conditions and a sustainable balance of payments'.

Member States are required to treat their economic policies 'as a matter of common concern' (Article 121(1) TFEU) and provision is made for their economic performance to be monitored by the Commission, the Council, and the European Council. The Council issues broad guidelines of economic policy for the Member States and the EU, although they are not legally binding.

Member States must also 'avoid excessive government deficits' (Article 126(1) TFEU). Compliance with this obligation is monitored by the Commission, which may if necessary enlist the support of the Council. The Council may ultimately require a Member State to reduce its deficit within a specified deadline (Article 126(9) TFEU). However, none of these obligations may be enforced by the Commission through infringement proceedings before the Court of Justice (Article 126(10) TFEU). Instead, where an excessive deficit persists, the Council may impose sanctions on the Member State concerned. These may include requiring it to make a non-interest-bearing deposit with the EU of a sum of money or to pay a fine. However, where the Council lacks the political will to act, it cannot be forced to do so. This was vividly illustrated in 2004, when the Commission unsuccessfully challenged the failure of the Council to act against excessive deficits in Germany and France (*Commission v Council* (2004)). The sanctions regime of Article 126 has yet to be used.

Responsibility for conducting monetary policy in the eurozone belongs to the ECB, which enjoys a high degree of independence: it may not take or seek instructions from EU institutions, the Member States, or any other body. The EU and the Member States undertake to respect this principle and not to seek to influence the ECB in the performance of its tasks (Article 130 TFEU). The ECB has law-making powers (Article 132 TFEU) and must be consulted on proposed EU acts and some national acts within its field of competence (Article 127(4) TFEU).

The ECB works with the central banks of all the Member States (whether or not they have adopted the euro) within the framework of the European System of Central Banks (ESCB). Article 127(1) TFEU says that 'The primary objective of the [ESCB] shall be to maintain price stability.' A tighter group known as the Eurosystem provides a forum for discussion between the ECB and the central banks of States which have adopted the euro.

The ECB has the exclusive right to authorize the issue of euro banknotes within the EU (Article 128(1) TFEU). The ECB and the national central banks are not permitted to offer credit facilities to EU institutions or bodies, central governments, or public authorities or to purchase debt from them (Article 123(1) TFEU). Neither the EU nor the Member States may be liable for the commitments of another Member State (Article 125(1) TFEU). These provisions reflect the original idea that eurozone members would be responsible for their own debts and would pursue economic policies that enabled them to borrow at reasonable rates of interest.

Nineteen Member States now belong to the eurozone (see Box 8). The UK and Denmark negotiated opt-outs at Maastricht, which enabled them to apply for membership if they wished to join. The remaining Member States (known as Member States with a derogation) are obliged to join if their economies are judged to have passed certain economic and political tests known as convergence criteria (see Article 140 TFEU and Protocol No. 13). Sweden, however, voted against joining in a referendum on 14 September 2003. To maintain confidence in the euro, membership is meant to be irreversible. The Treaties seem to contemplate only one way out: withdrawal from the EU entirely.

Box 8 Members of the eurozone

Member State	Date of entry
Austria	1 January 1999
Belgium	1 January 1999
Cyprus	1 January 2008
Estonia	1 January 2011
Finland	1 January 1999
France	1 January 1999
Germany	1 January 1999
Greece	1 January 2001
Ireland	1 January 1999
Italy	1 January 1999
Latvia	1 January 2014
Lithuania	1 January 2015
Luxembourg	1 January 1999
Malta	1 January 2008
The Netherlands	1 January 1999
Portugal	1 January 1999
Slovakia	1 January 2009
Slovenia	1 January 2007
Spain	1 January 1999

A flaw in this system which immediately attracted criticism is the rupture it creates between two aspects of a State's economic policy. One is monetary policy (printing money, setting interest rates, and the like), where the EU enjoys exclusive competence for Member States in the eurozone (Article 3(1)(c) TFEU). The other is fiscal policy (raising money and deciding how to spend it), which is conducted at national level. This weakness was exacerbated by the EU's failure to employ the excessive deficit procedure with sufficient rigour and to apply with due diligence the convergence criteria when deciding whether to admit Member States to the eurozone.

A fire was kindled under the eurozone in the period leading up to the financial crash of 2008, when lenders allowed all Member States whose currency was the euro to borrow money at broadly comparable cost. This led some Member States to borrow excessive amounts. The crash caused lenders to focus on members of the eurozone individually. The result was that for some of them, such as Ireland, Portugal, and Greece, the cost of borrowing money soared, causing budget deficits to rise to unsustainable levels. Eventually they faced the prospect of being unable to borrow at all and having to default on their debts. They were unable to make their exports more competitive or attract extra tourists by devaluing their currencies because the value of the euro is common to all Member States that have adopted it.

Considering it essential to preserve the integrity of the eurozone, the EU offered financial assistance to members in difficulty. The objective was to prevent them from defaulting on their debts and being forced out of the eurozone and possibly the EU itself. There was also a resolve to avoid 'contagion', where the markets picked off weaker economies one by one and made it more difficult to maintain the credibility of the euro.

Together with the International Monetary Fund (IMF), an international organization which helps to resolve international financial crises, the EU therefore embarked on a programme of what came to be known as bailouts. To qualify for assistance, States in difficulty were expected to agree to reform their economies to prevent a recurrence of the circumstances in which they found themselves. At the outset, this process seemed to work reasonably well but Greece stretched it almost to breaking point as the conditions attached to successive bailouts led to unemployment, poverty, and public disorder.

Moreover, the process exposed the EU to the familiar criticism that it lacked democratic legitimacy, because it appeared that economic policy in recipient States was being dictated by the so-called troika of the European Commission, the ECB, and the IMF, bypassing democratically elected governments. To critics of this persuasion, Greece provided the most telling example. The Syriza government of Alexis Tsipras was elected in January 2015 on a platform of opposition to the austerity which previous bailout conditions had caused. The strict conditions attached to a later bailout were rejected in a national referendum on 5 July 2015 but essentially accepted just days later to avoid a Greek exit from the eurozone, for which Tsipras felt he had no mandate. His approach was vindicated in September 2015, when Syriza won a second election, albeit with a slightly reduced share of the vote.

Some of the criticism heaped on the troika is unfair. Greece concealed the true state of its finances after gaining admission to the eurozone in 2001. Its economic predicament when the crash came was 'the result of sovereign decisions taken by successive elected governments over the years', as Natalie Nougayrède pointed out in *The Guardian* on 19 June 2015. The other members of the eurozone were constrained in what they could do by their own electorates. On the other hand, much of the bailout money nominally received by Greece went straight to its creditors, some of which were banks located elsewhere in the eurozone, particularly Germany. The conditions imposed on Greece plunged its already weak economy into freefall, making it ever less likely that it would be able to recover. Even the IMF was driven to admit that Greece's debts had become unsustainable and that debt relief would have to be considered.

The eurozone crisis confronted the EU with an existential dilemma. It shattered public confidence in its economic competence. It undermined its pretensions to solidarity among its members. It reinforced criticism of its democratic legitimacy. It fuelled the rise of nationalist parties across Europe. It drove a wedge between France and Germany, so long the motor of European integration but who took divergent views on Greece. Yanis Varoufakis, the former Greek Finance Minister, claimed in *The Guardian* on 11 July 2015 that the German Finance Minister wanted Greece 'to be pushed out of the single currency to put the fear of God into the French and have them accept his model of a disciplinarian eurozone'.

Some who took this view would have sacrificed the euro in order to preserve the EU, whose survival they believed to be threatened. On the other hand, French President François Hollande maintained in *Le Journal du dimanche* on 19 July 2015 that the problem lay not in too much Europe but in too little. He advocated a government for the eurozone with its own budget and parliament. Jürgen Habermas, the German philosopher, argued in *The Guardian* on 16 July 2015 that the solution lay in 'a more strongly integrated "core Europe"'.

Time will tell how this debate over the soul of the EU pans out. Opposing views were voiced by some of the newer Member States following the UK referendum in June 2016. There may also be resistance from some national courts. In its *Lisbon* decision of 30 June 2009, the Bundesverfassungsgericht said that the right to take 'fundamental fiscal decisions on public revenue and expenditure' formed part of Germany's 'constitutional identity' and could not be surrendered to the EU in the absence of democratic representation of the kind normally found in a State.

The legal framework for the EU's responses to the crisis was varied and sometimes ingenious. The only Treaty provision which envisaged the provision of EU financial assistance was Article 122(2) TFEU, according to which such assistance could be provided by the Council where a Member State 'is in difficulties or is seriously threatened by natural disasters or exceptional occurrences beyond its control…'. The urgency and the difficulty of securing agreement among all twenty-eight Member States required Treaty changes to be kept to an absolute minimum. Instead, a mixture of classical legal instruments, international agreements between eurozone members outside the framework of the EU, and ECB decisions was employed.

The legal response began in 2010 with the establishment of temporary mechanisms to assist members of the eurozone in financial difficulty. The first was the European Financial Stability Mechanism (EFSM), set up by Council regulation under Article 122(2) TFEU to provide a temporary financial assistance mechanism. The EFSM was complemented by a more powerful mechanism known as the European Financial Stability Facility (EFSF). Established by international agreement, this made the members of the eurozone shareholders in a private company established in Luxembourg to grant loans to members in difficulty. In addition, the ECB adopted a decision in 2010 establishing a securities markets programme (SMP) enabling it to purchase bonds issued by eurozone members on the secondary markets, where such bonds are traded by investors.

In March 2011, a decision was adopted by the European Council under the simplified revision procedure set out in Article 48(6) TEU. That decision inserted into Article 136 TFEU a new paragraph permitting eurozone members to 'establish a stability mechanism to be activated if indispensable to safeguard the stability of the euro area as a whole'. The granting of financial assistance under that mechanism was to be made subject to strict conditions.

Before that decision had entered into force, the eurozone Member States concluded the European Stability Mechanism (ESM) Treaty, which created a new international financial institution to provide a permanent mechanism for providing assistance to eurozone Member States facing severe financing problems. The ESM Treaty gives the Court of Justice the right to interpret and apply its provisions. This is permitted by Article 273 TFEU, which confers on the Court of Justice jurisdiction 'in any dispute between Member States which relates to the subject matter of the Treaties if the dispute is submitted to it under a special agreement between the parties'.

In the *Pringle* case, one of the questions raised was whether the ESM Treaty could lawfully be concluded before the decision of the European Council amending Article 136 had taken effect. The Court of Justice said it could, because the amendment merely confirmed a power already possessed by the Member States. That pragmatic conclusion was probably justified given the extraordinary circumstances.

A more far-reaching set of Treaty changes was blocked by the UK in December 2011, ostensibly over the refusal of other Member States to grant the UK concessions on financial markets regulation. The changes were instead embodied in a Treaty on Stability, Coordination, and Governance in the EMU or 'Fiscal Compact' signed in March 2012 by all the then Member States except the UK and the Czech Republic.

The Fiscal Compact requires the Contracting Parties to introduce binding provisions ensuring that their budgets are 'balanced or in surplus'. A form of infringement procedure is available to enforce that requirement, enabling Contracting Parties to bring proceedings before the Court of Justice against each other if it is breached. The Court of Justice may impose financial sanctions on any Contracting Party which fails to comply with a judgment against it under this procedure. Recourse to the Court of Justice is possible because the relevant provision is said to constitute 'a special agreement between the Contracting Parties within the meaning of Article 273 [TFEU]'.

As the crisis developed and investors lost confidence in the survival of the euro, some Member States encountered difficulty in selling bonds at reasonable rates of interest. In a widely quoted remark, the President of the ECB said in July 2012 that it was 'ready to do whatever it takes to preserve the euro'. The following September, the ECB issued a press release announcing its intention to launch a scheme of so-called outright monetary transactions (OMTs) to replace the SMP. OMTs would involve the unlimited purchase by the ESCB on secondary markets of government bonds issued by eurozone members which were subject to financial support under the EFSF or the ESM.

Although the legal acts necessary to give effect to the scheme had not yet been adopted, a series of constitutional actions was brought before the Bundesverfassungsgericht on a preventive basis in which the power of the ESCB to adopt such a scheme was challenged. The Bundesverfassungsgericht for the first time ever made a reference to the Court of Justice for a preliminary ruling under Article 267 TFEU, indicating that it was minded to find the scheme unlawful and incompatible with Germany's constitutional identity. However, the Court of Justice found that the scheme fell within the scope of the powers conferred on the ESCB by the Treaty (*Gauweiler and Others v Deutscher Bundestag* (2015)). At the time of the judgment, the scheme had still to be mplemented but its very announcement had calmed the markets and allowed governments to borrow at more reasonable rates.

o this complicated mosaic must be added the 'Six Pack' and the wo Pack'. These were bundles of conventional EU acts adopted 2011 and 2013 respectively. Their purpose was to reinforce onomic surveillance and coordination in the eurozone and make easier to impose fines on Member States which ran up excessive deficits. In addition, the European Council agreed in 2012 to create a 'banking union' with three elements: a 'single rulebook' comprising legislative texts binding on all financial institutions in the EU; a Single Supervisory Mechanism (SSM) making the ECB the main supervisor of financial institutions in the eurozone; and a Single Resolution Mechanism (SRM) to make it easier for bank failures to be tackled. Participation in the SSM and the SRM was to be compulsory for members of the eurozone and optional for other Member States.

The so-called 'Five Presidents' Report' published by the Commission in June 2015 set out ambitious plans for completing EMU by 2025. They included boosting competitiveness and convergence between Member States; improved democratic accountability; greater emphasis on employment and social concerns; the creation of a eurozone treasury as a forum for collective decision-making on fiscal policy; and integrating intergovernmental arrangements into the framework of EU law. In the longer term, the transfer to the EU of control over economic and fiscal policy was contemplated. This would test the limits of the EU's democratic legitimacy.

The migration crisis

With the eurozone crisis still unresolved, in 2015 the EU was confronted with an influx of over a million migrants from Syria, Afghanistan, and elsewhere arriving via the Mediterranean and western Balkans. The migrants' plight was captured by a shocking image of a dead Syrian toddler, Alan Kurdi, washed up on a Turkish beach. The 'open door' policy of Chancellor Angela Merkel led many of them to seek refuge in Germany (see Figure 8). However, it caused dismay in other Schengen States, who saw it as encouraging further migration. Some of them reintroduced border controls and resorted to water cannon and tear gas to repel migrants. The crisis put severe pressure on the system for determining the Member State responsible for

8. CJEU President Vassilios Skouris welcomes German Chancellor Angela Merkel, a key figure in the migration crisis (9 March 2010).

examining applications for asylum established by the so-called Dublin III Regulation.

Article 78(3) TFEU enables the EU to act where a Member State is 'confronted by an emergency situation characterised by a sudden inflow of nationals of third countries'. In September 2015, the Council adopted two decisions to relocate 160,000 people in need of international protection to other Member States for the benefit of Italy and Greece, who were under exceptional pressure. Because of their opt-outs from the AFSJ, the UK, Ireland, and Denmark did not participate in these measures, though Ireland agreed to take some migrants on a voluntary basis.

The second of those decisions was adopted by qualified majority vote in the teeth of opposition from the Czech Republic, Slovakia, Hungary, and Romania. Slovakia announced that it would challenge its legality in the Court of Justice. Following the terrorist attacks in Paris on 13 November 2015 and suspicions that the perpetrators included migrants, Slovakia and Poland declared the relocation plan no longer viable and Hungary said it too would challenge it before the Court of Justice. On 2 October 2016, the relocation plan was rejected by a majority of 98 per cent in a referendum of the Hungarian people, although the turnout of 43 per cent fell short of the 50 per cent validity threshold.

Meanwhile the EU attempted to make progress on other fronts, such as drawing up a list of countries to which those seeking asylum could safely be returned and reforming Dublin III. It extended the mandate of Frontex by establishing a European border and coast guard. It also sought to cooperate more closely with Turkey, a key transit route for migrants travelling to Europe.

To disrupt the activities of people smugglers, on 18 March 2016 the EU agreed a so-called statement with Turkey. This provided that irregular migrants crossing from that country to Greece would be returned and that, for every Syrian returned to Turkey from Greece, another Syrian would be resettled in the EU. Those applying for asylum in Greece would be considered individually. Member States agreed to provide Greece with human, material, and financial support, including border guards, interpreters, asylum specialists, boats, and buses. For its part, the EU would make a significant financial contribution to the cost of managing migrants in Turkey, lift the visa requirements for Turkish citizens travelling within the Schengen area, and restart stalled negotiations on Turkey's membership of the EU.

These arrangements immediately attracted criticism on humanitarian grounds. In a sign of disapproval, Pope Francis visited the Greek island of Lesbos in April 2016 and returned to the Vatican with twelve migrants. While the scheme significantly reduced the flow of migrants via Turkey, doubts about its future were raised by the response of the Turkish Government to the failed coup of 15 July 2016. Meanwhile the route from Libya to Italy remained problematic.

The future?

The eurozone and migration crises unmasked an EU apparently devoid of solidarity and riven instead by north–south and east–west divides, where adherence to its 'values' was only skin-deep. It has been further weakened by the desire of one of its most powerful members to withdraw, a symptom of a deeper malaise. In his State of the Union address to the European Parliament on 14 September 2016, the President of the Commission acknowledged the seriousness of the crisis facing the EU and bemoaned the lack of common ground between Member States. Some argue that the solution is deeper integration, others that the EU should pay more attention to the wishes of its Member States.

On 16 September 2016, the HoSG of twenty-seven of the Member States met in Bratislava in the absence of the UK. In a declaration issued after the meeting, the leaders of the twenty-seven said that '[t]he EU is not perfect but it is the best instrument we have for addressing the new challenges we are facing'. They recognized the importance of 'challenging simplistic solutions of extreme or populist political forces' and set out a roadmap of practical steps to be taken in areas like border control, security, and the economy. Whatever is ultimately agreed, there is no doubt that the law will have a vital role to play in putting it into effect.

References

General

Since the entry into force of the Treaty of Lisbon in December 2009, the term European Union or EU has embraced the mechanisms for cooperation formerly known as the EEC, the common market, or the European Community. I have used the term EU even when discussing developments before the Treaty of Lisbon, except where it was necessary to refer specifically to an earlier version of the Treaties.

The provisions of the Treaties are known as articles. Article 36 EEC means Article 36 of the Treaty establishing the European Economic Community; Article 2 TEU means Article 2 of the Treaty on European Union; Article 263 TFEU means Article 263 of the Treaty on the Functioning of the European Union.

The TEU and the TFEU feature a number of attachments called protocols. These 'form an integral part' of the Treaties to which they belong. They have the same legal status as the Treaties themselves and form part of the EU's primary law.

So-called COM (or communication) documents may be found at <http://eur-lex.europa.eu/collection/eu-law/pre-acts.html?locale=en> (accessed 19 September 2016) or by searching their number online, e.g. COM(2015) 240 final.

Introduction

The quotation is taken from the preamble to the ECSC Treaty.

Chapter 1: What is EU law about?

For criticism of the *Mangold* case by a former President of Germany,
see Roman Herzog and Lüder Gerken, 'Stop the European Court of
Justice' (Freiburg, Centrum für Europäische Politik, 2008).

The quotation from Takis Tridimas may be found in *The General
Principles of EU Law* (Oxford, OUP, 2nd edn, 2006), 139.

The quotation from Stefan Enchelmaier may be found in Peter Oliver
(ed.), *Oliver on Free Movement of Goods in the European Union*
(Oxford, Hart, 5th edn, 2010), 215, 216.

The quotation from Jukka Snell may be found in P. Craig and
G. de Búrca (eds), *The Evolution of EU Law* (Oxford, OUP, 2nd edn,
2011), 547, 574.

Chapter 2: From Common Market to European Union

The case of Rachid Ramda was mentioned by the then UK Home
Secretary Theresa May in a speech in London on 25 April 2016:
<https://www.gov.uk/government/speeches/home-secretarys-
speech-on-the-uk-eu-and-our-place-in-the-world> (accessed
19 September 2016).

The quotation from Steve Peers may be found in *EU Justice and Home
Affairs Law* (Oxford, OUP, 3rd edn, 2011), 859.

The quotations from the House of Lords EU Committee may be found
in 'EU Police and Criminal Justice Measures: The UK's 2014
Opt-Out Decision' (13th Report of Session 2012–13, HL Paper
159), paras 76 and 79.

For litigation over the right of the UK to opt in to elements of
the Schengen acquis, see e.g. Case C-77/05 *United Kingdom v
Council* EU:C:2007:803; Case C-137/05 *United Kingdom v Council*
EU:C:2007:805; Case C-482/08 *United Kingdom v Council*
EU:C:2010:631.

For the list of AFSJ measures the UK opted back in to, see Decision
2014/858, OJ 2014 L 345/6.

For the UK's balance of competences review, see <https://www.gov.uk/
review-of-the-balance-of-competences> (accessed 19 September
2016). For a report on the review by the House of Lords EU
Committee, see 'The Review of the Balance of Competences
between the UK and the EU' (12th Report of Session 2014–15, HL
Paper 140).

Chapter 3: Secondary EU law

For analysis of voting patterns in the European Parliament, see VoteWatch.eu, 'Voting in the 2009–2014 European Parliament: How do MEPs Vote after Lisbon?' (3rd report) <http://www.votewatch.eu/blog/wp-content/uploads/2011/01/votewatch_report_voting_behavior_26_january_beta.pdf)> (accessed 19 September 2016).

Nigel Farage's remark about Herman van Rompuy was made in the European Parliament on 24 February 2010.

Henry Kissinger was National Security Advisor and Secretary of State under former US Presidents Richard Nixon and Gerald Ford.

The permanent representatives of the Member States are distinct from the ambassadors who head the embassies maintained by each Member State in Brussels.

On the concessions extracted by Poland and Spain, see Article 3 of Protocol (No. 36) on Transitional Provisions, annexed to the TEU and the TFEU; Council Decision of 13 December 2007 relating to the implementation of Article 9C(4) of the Treaty on European Union and Article 205(2) of the Treaty on the Functioning of the European Union between 1 November 2014 and 31 March 2017 on the one hand, and as from 1 April 2017 on the other, OJ 2009 L 314/73.

The increasing size of the Commission gave rise to concerns that its effectiveness might be impaired. Article 17(5) TEU therefore envisaged that, with effect from 1 November 2014, the number of Commissioners should correspond to only two-thirds of the number of Member States. The European Council was given the power to alter that number. The loss of a permanent Commissioner became an issue in the first Irish referendum on the Lisbon Treaty (see Chapter 5). The European Council therefore agreed that the Commission would for the time being continue to include a national from each Member State.

For the report of the special committee on the LuxLeaks affair, see European Parliament resolution of 25 November 2015 on tax rulings and other measures similar in nature or effect, 2015/2966 (INI); 'Parliament's committees of enquiry and special committees' (European Parliamentary Research Service, June 2016, PE 582.007), 13–14.

The report of the Committee of Independent Experts was entitled *First Report on Allegations Regarding Fraud, Mismanagement and Nepotism in the European Commission* and was published on 15 March 1999. A second report, entitled *Reform of the*

Commission: Analysis of Current Practice and Proposals for Tackling Mismanagement, Irregularities and Fraud, was published on 10 September 1999.

The Commission's work programme for 2016 was entitled 'No time for business as usual' (COM(2015) 610 final, 27 October 2015).

Chapter 4: How secondary EU law is made

On trilogues, see Decision of the European Ombudsman setting out proposals following her strategic inquiry OI/8/2015/JAS concerning the transparency of Trilogues (12 July 2016) <http://www.ombudsman.europa.eu/cases/decision.faces/en/69206/html.bookmark> (accessed 19 September 2016).

The regulation on the supervision of implementing powers is Regulation 182/2011 of the European Parliament and of the Council of 16 February 2011 laying down the rules and general principles concerning mechanisms for control by Member States of the Commission's exercise of implementing powers, OJ 2011 L 55/13.

Commission President Juncker's remarks on interference by the EU in the lives of its citizens and subsidiarity were made at a meeting of parliamentarians in Strasbourg on 19 April 2016.

On REFIT, see 'EU Regulatory Fitness' (COM(2012) 746 final, 12 December 2012). More information on 'better regulation' generally is available at <http://ec.europa.eu/info/strategy/better-regulation-why-and-how_en> (accessed 19 September 2016).

On enlisting the help of national parliaments, see Protocol No. 2 on the application of the principles of subsidiarity and proportionality; House of Lords EU Committee, 'The role of national parliaments in the European Union' (9th report of session 2013–14, HL Paper 151).

The first quotation from Joseph Weiler may be found in *The Constitution of Europe* (Cambridge, CUP, 1999), 266. The second and third may be found in Julie Dickson and Pavlos Eleftheriadis (eds), *Philosophical Foundations of European Union Law* (Oxford, OUP, 2012), 137, 140–1, and 142 respectively.

On input and output legitimacy, see Fritz Scharpf, *Governing in Europe: Effective and Democratic?* (Oxford, OUP, 1999), 6–13.

Chapter 5: On the origin of treaties

For a detailed study of the use of referendums in the EU, see
Fernando Mendez, Mario Mendez, and Vasiliki Triga, *Referendums
and the European Union: A Comparative Enquiry* (Cambridge,
CUP, 2014).

The quotation from Allan Tatham may be found in Andrea Biondi,
Piet Eeckhout, and Stefanie Ripley (eds), *EU Law after Lisbon*
(Oxford, OUP, 2012), 128, 139.

Norway belongs to the European Economic Area (EEA). See <http://
www.efta.int/> (accessed 19 September 2016).

The quotations from Christophe Hillion may be found in Anthony
Arnull and Damian Chalmers (eds), *The Oxford Handbook of
European Union Law* (Oxford, OUP, 2015), 126, 129, and 149
respectively.

For analysis by the British Government of the withdrawal process, see
The Process for Withdrawing from the European Union (Cm 9216,
February 2016).

The text of the settlement reached with the UK was annexed to
the Conclusions of the European Council meeting of 18 and
19 February 2016 (<http://data.consilium.europa.eu/doc/document/
ST-1-2016-INIT/en/pdf> (accessed 19 September 2016)).

The first referendum on Scottish independence took place on
18 September 2014. Independence was rejected by a majority
of 55.3 per cent of the votes cast.

Chapter 6: EU law in the national courts

The quotations from Hjalte Rasmussen may be found in *On Law and
Policy in the European Court of Justice: A Comparative Study in
Judicial Policymaking* (Dordrecht, Martinus Nijhoff, 1986), 28
and 12 respectively.

The quotation from Stephen Weatherill may be found in *Law and
Integration in the European Union* (Oxford, OUP, 1995), 124.

The quotation from Sionaidh Douglas-Scott may be found in
Constitutional Law of the European Union (Harlow, Longman,
2002), 322.

The quotation from Sir Neil MacCormick may be found in
*Questioning Sovereignty: Law, State, and Nation in the European
Commonwealth* (Oxford, OUP, 1999), 119–20.

Chapter 7: The Court of Justice of the European Union

Statistics on the CJEU's judicial activity are available on its website: <http://curia.europa.eu/> (accessed 19 September 2016).

For the pressures on the EU court system, see House of Lords EU Committee, 'The Workload of the Court of Justice of the European Union' (Session 2010–11, 14th Report, HL Paper 128) and 'Workload of the Court of Justice of the European Union: Follow-Up Report' (Session 2012–13, 16th Report, HL Paper 163).

On increasing the size of the General Court, see Regulation 2015/2422 of the European Parliament and the Council of 16 December 2015 amending Protocol No. 3 on the Statute of the Court of Justice of the European Union, OJ 2015 L 341/14.

The quotation from the House of Lords EU Committee on the best background for senior judicial office may be found in '1996 Inter-Governmental Conference' (Session 1994–5, 21st Report, HL Paper 105), para. 260.

The quotation on 'creative jurisprudence' may be found in Sir Patrick Neill, *The European Court of Justice: A Case Study in Judicial Activism* (European Policy Forum/Frankfurter Institut, August 1995), 1.

Chapter 8: Enforcing EU law

For the Commission's priorities in infringement proceedings, see 'White Paper on European Governance' COM(2001) 428 final; 'Better Governance for the Single Market' COM(2012) 259 final.

For the Commission's 2015 report, see 'Monitoring the Application of European Union Law: 2015 Annual Report' COM(2016) 463 final, 25–31.

On the controversy surrounding the Polish Constitutional Court, see the report of the Venice Commission (the Council of Europe's advisory body on constitutional affairs) of 11 March 2016 (Opinion no. 833/2015). The intervention of the Commission took place under the rule of law framework set out in COM(2014) 158 final (19 March 2014).

The quotation from David Anderson QC and Marie Demetriou QC may be found in *References to the European Court* (London, Sweet & Maxwell, 2nd edn, 2002), 327–30.

The quotation from Judge Pescatore may be found in Miguel Poiares Maduro and Loïc Azoulai (eds), *The Past and Future of EU Law* (Oxford, Hart, 2010), 6.

On the subversion of national judicial hierarchies, see further Joseph
   Weiler, *The Constitution of Europe* (Cambridge, CUP, 1999), 197;
   Karen Alter, *Establishing the Supremacy of European Law*
   (Oxford, OUP, 2001), 45–52.

Chapter 9: Coping with crises

The 'Five Presidents' are the Presidents of the European Commission;
   the Euro Summit (comprising the HoSG of the euro area
   countries, the Euro Summit President and the President of the
   Commission); the Euro Group (comprising the finance ministers
   of the euro area); the ECB; and the European Parliament. Their
   report, entitled *Completing Europe's Economic and Monetary
   Union*, is available at <http://ec.europa.eu/priorities/publications/
   five-presidents-report-completing-europes-economic-and-monetary-
   union_en> (accessed 19 September 2016).
The Dublin III Regulation is Regulation 604/2013 establishing the
   criteria and mechanisms for determining the Member State
   responsible for examining an application for international
   protection lodged in one of the Member States by a third-country
   national or a stateless person, OJ 2013 L 180/31.
The relocation measures adopted in September 2015 are Decision
   2015/1523 establishing provisional measures in the area of
   international protection for the benefit of Italy and of Greece, OJ
   2015 L 239/146 and Decision 2015/1601 establishing provisional
   measures in the area of international protection for the benefit of
   Italy and Greece, OJ 2015 L 248/80.
For the text of the EU–Turkey statement, see <http://www.consilium.
   europa.eu/en/press/press-releases/2016/03/18-eu-turkey-statement/>
   (accessed 19 September 2016).
On the difficulties posed by the migration route from Libya to Italy,
   see House of Lords EU Committee, 'Operation Sophia, the EU's
   Naval Mission in the Mediterranean: An Impossible Challenge'
   (14th Report of Session 2015–16, HL Paper 144).

List of cases and EU measures

List of cases

If you want to read a judgment of the CJEU or an Opinion of an Advocate General, where can they be found? Until 2011, judgments and Opinions were published in hard copy in all the official languages of the EU in the *European Court Reports*. These may be found in all good law libraries. Since 2012, judgments and Opinions have been available online only. They can be found on the website of the CJEU, where there is a basic search facility: see <http://curia.europa.eu/> (accessed 19 September 2016). However, if you know the relevant case number or European Case Law Identifier (ECLI), the easiest thing to do is to search one or the other online. You will then be taken directly to the judgment or Opinion on the website of the CJEU.

The list below will enable those who are interested to locate the text of all the judgments of the CJEU referred to in this book. It is arranged alphabetically. Each case name is followed by the case number (e.g. Case C-617/10) and the ECLI (e.g. EU:C:2013:105). The prefix 'C-' before the case number denotes a case decided by the Court of Justice, the prefix 'T-' a case decided by the General Court. Where there is no prefix, the case was decided before the General Court was established.

The list is followed by a list of the decisions of national courts referred to in this book. They may be found through online databases (though some of these may be subscription-only) and in good law libraries.

Court of Justice of the European Union

Åkerberg Fransson Case C-617/10 EU:C:2013:105

Alpine Investments Case C-384/93 EU:C:1995:126

Angelidaki Joined Cases C-378/07 to C-380/07 EU:C:2009:250

Antonissen Case C-292/89 EU:C:1991:80

Aranyosi and Căldăraru Joined Cases C-404/15 and C-659/15
    EU:C:2016:198

Audiolux Case C-101/08 EU:C:2009:626

Baumbast and R Case C-413/99 EU:C:2002:493

Bosman Case C-415/93 EU:C:1995:463

Brasserie du Pêcheur and Factortame Joined Cases C-46/93 and
    C-48/93 EU:C:1996:79

'Cassis de Dijon' (*Rewe-Zentral AG v Bundesmonopolverwaltung für
    Branntwein*) Case 120/78 EU:C:1979:42

CILFIT v Ministry of Health Case 283/81 EU:C:1982:335

Commission v Belgium Case 77/69 EU:C:1970:34

Commission v Belgium Case 149/79 EU:C:1980:297

Commission v Council Case C-27/04 EU:C:2004:436

Commission v Cresson Case C-432/04 EU:C:2006:455

Commission v France Case C-265/95 EU:C:1997:595

Commission v France Case C-304/02 EU:C:2005:444

Commission v Germany Case 178/84 EU:C:1987:126

Commission v Greece Case C-387/97 EU:C:2000:356

Commission v Ireland Case 249/81 EU:C:1982:402

Commission v Luxembourg and Belgium Joined Cases 90 and 91/63
    EU:C:1964:80

Commission v United Kingdom Case 170/78 EU:C:1983:202

Commission v United Kingdom Case C-98/01 EU:C:2003:273

Consten and Grundig v Commission Joined Cases 56 and 58/64
    EU:C:1966:41

Costa v ENEL Case 6/64 EU:C:1964:66

Council v Commission Case C-409/13 EU:C:2015:217

Dalli v Commission Case T-562/12 EU:T:2015:270

Dano Case C-333/13 EU:C:2014:2358

Defrenne v SABENA (*Defrenne II*) Case 43/75 EU:C:1976:56

Deutsche Telekom v Schröder Case C-50/96 EU:C:2000:72

Dominguez v CICOA Case C-282/10 EU:C:2012:33

Faccini Dori v Recreb Case C-91/92 EU:C:1994:292

FII Group Litigation Case C-446/04 EU:C:2006:774

Foster Case C–188/89 EU:C:1990:313

Foto-Frost v Hauptzollamt Lübeck-Ost Case 314/85 EU:C:1987:452

Francovich Joined Cases C-6/90 and C-9/90 EU:C:1991:428

Gaston Schul Douane-Expediteur Case C-461/03 EU:C:2005:742

Gauweiler and Others v Deutscher Bundestag Case C-62/14
    EU:C:2015:400

Gebhard Case C-55/94 EU:C:1995:41

Germany v Council ('Tobacco Advertising case') Case C-376/98
    EU:C:2000:544

Google Spain v AEPD Case C-131/12 EU:C:2014:317

Grad v Finanzamt Traunstein Case 9/70 EU:C:1970:78

Greenpeace and Others v Commission Case C-321/95 P
    EU:C:1998:153

Grzelczyk C-184/99 EU:C:2001:458

Inter-Environnement Wallonie v Région Wallonne Case C-41/11
    EU:C:2012:103

*Internationale Handelsgesellschaft v Einfuhr- und Vorratsstelle
    Getreide* Case 11/70 EU:C:1970:114

*Inuit Tapiriit Kanatami and Others v European Parliament and
    Council* Case T-18/10 [2011] ECR II-5599 EU:C:2013:625

Josemans Case C-137/09 EU:C:2010:774

Kadi and Another v Council and Commission Joined Cases C-402/05
    P and C-415/05 P EU:C:2008:461

Keck and Mithouard Joined Cases C-267/91 and C-268/91
    EU:C:1993:905

Kerckhaert Case C-513/04 EU:C:2006:713

Köbler v Austria Case C-224/01 EU:C:2003:513

Kone AG and Others v ÖBB-Infrastruktur AG Case C-557/12
    EU:C:2014:1317

Križan Case C-416/10 EU:C:2013:8

Kücükdeveci Case C-555/07 EU:C:2010:21

Laval Case C-341/05 EU:C:2007:809

Ledra Advertising Joined Cases C-8/15 P to C-10/15 P
    EU:C:2016:701

Luisi and Carbone v Ministero del Tesoro Joined Cases 286/82 and
    26/83 EU:C:1984:35

Mangold Case C-144/04 EU:C:2005:709

*Marshall v Southampton and South-West Hampshire Area Health
    Authority* Case 152/84 EU:C:1986:84

Melloni Case C-399/11 EU:C:2013:107

Microsoft v Commission Case T-201/04 EU:T:2007:289

NCC Construction Danmark Case C-174/08 EU:C:2009:669

Plaumann v Commission Case 25/62 EU:C:1963:17

PPG and SNF v European Chemicals Agency Case C-626/11
    EU:C:2013:595

Pringle v Government of Ireland Case C-370/12 EU:C:2012:756

Rau v De Smedt Case 261/81 EU:C:1982:382

Reyners v Belgium Case 2/74 EU:C:1974:68

Römer Case C-147/08 EU:C:2011:286

Roquette Frères v Council Case 138/79 EU:C:1980:249

Ruiz Zambrano Case C-34/09 EU:C:2011:124

Sapod Audic Case C-159/00 EU:C:2002:343

SDDDA v Commission Case T-47/96 EU:T:1996:164

Spain and Italy v Council Joined Cases C-274/11 and C-295/11
    EU:C:2013:240

Stauder v Ulm Case 29/69 EU:C:1969:57

Stichting Woonpunt Case C-132/12 P EU:C:2014:100

Torfaen Borough Council v B&Q Case C-145/88 EU:C:1989:593

TWD Textilwerke Deggendorf Case C-188/92 EU:C:1994:90

United Kingdom v Council Case C-84/94 EU:C:1996:431

Van Binsbergen v Bedrijfsvereniging Metaalnijverheid Case 33/74
    EU:C:1974:131

Van Gend en Loos v Nederlandse Administratie der Belastingen Case
    26/62 EU:C:1963:1

Variola Case 34/73 EU:C:1973:101

Viking Case C-438/05 EU:C:2007:772

Zhu and Chen v Secretary of State Case C-200/02 EU:C:2004:639

Opinions of the Court of Justice under Article 218(11) TFEU on the compatibility with EU law of international agreements which the EU is proposing to conclude

Opinion 2/94 Accession by the EC to the European Convention for the
    Protection of Human Rights and Fundamental Freedoms
    EU:C:1996:140

Opinion 1/09 Creation of a unified patent litigation system
    EU:C:2011:123

Opinion 2/13 EU Accession to the European Convention for the
    Protection of Human Rights and Fundamental Freedoms
    EU:C:2014:2454

National courts

Assange v The Swedish Prosecution Authority [2011] UKSC 22 (UK Supreme Court)

Brunner v European Union Treaty [1994] 1 Common Market Law Reports 57 (Bundesverfassungsgericht)

Cohn-Bendit [1980] 1 Common Market Law Reports 543 (French Conseil d'État)

Customs and Excise v Samex ApS [1983] 3 Common Market Law Reports 194 (English High Court)

Gauweiler, judgment of 21 June 2016 (Bundesverfassungsgericht)

Honeywell [2011] 1 Common Market Law Reports 33 (Bundesverfassungsgericht)

Internationale Handelsgesellschaft mbH v Einfuhr- und Vorratsstelle für Getreide und Futtermittel [1974] 2 Common Market Law Reports 540 (Bundesverfassungsgericht)

R (Miller) v Secretary of State [2017] UKSC 5

Re Ratification of the Treaty of Lisbon [2010] 3 Common Market Law Reports 13 (Bundesverfassungsgericht)

'Slovak Pensions' case Pl. ÚS 5/12, 31 January 2012 (Czech Constitutional Court)

Judgments of the UK Supreme Court are available here: <https://www.supremecourt.uk/> (accessed 19 September 2016)

Some judgments and press releases of the Bundesverfassungsgericht are available in English here: <http://www.bundesverfassungsgericht.de/EN/Homepage/home_node.html> (accessed 19 September 2016)

Some judgments of the Constitutional Court of the Czech Republic are available in English here: <http://www.usoud.cz/en/> (accessed 19 September 2016)

List of EU measures

Article 297 TFEU requires legislative acts, regulations, and directives which are addressed to all Member States, and decisions which do not specify any addressees, to be published in the Official Journal of the European Union (OJ), available online at <http://europa.eu/eu-law/legislation/index_en.htm> (accessed 19 September 2016). The OJ is an official gazette which contains (in the L series) the texts of EU acts and (in the C series) proposals and other non-binding documents. Acts which have to be published in the OJ enter into force on the date specified in them or, if no date is specified, on the twentieth day after publication.

This list gives details of the main acts of EU secondary law referred to in this book. The easiest way to locate an act is to search online for its number (where it has one) or its OJ reference, which shows respectively the year of publication, the series, the issue, and the page number. For the first measure mentioned in this list, this would mean searching either 'Regulation 1/2003' or 'OJ 2003 L 1/1'.

Because the titles of EU acts are often long and unwieldy, they are sometimes given nicknames. Examples are the 'Working Time Directive' and the 'Dublin III Regulation'. Such nicknames have no formal status and may not be used consistently.

Regulation 17 of 6 February 1962, first regulation implementing Articles 85 and 86 of the Treaty, OJ Special Edition 1959–62, p. 87.

Council Regulation 1/2003 of 16 December 2002 on the implementation of the rules on competition laid down in Articles 81 and 82 of the Treaty.

Council Regulation 407/2010 of 11 May 2010 establishing a European financial stabilization mechanism, OJ 2010 L 118/1.

Regulation 182/2011 of the European Parliament and of the Council of 16 February 2011 laying down the rules and general principles concerning mechanisms for control by Member States of the Commission's exercise of implementing powers, OJ 2011 L 55/13.

Regulation 604/2013 of the European Parliament and of the Council of 26 June 2013 establishing the criteria and mechanisms for determining the Member State responsible for examining an application for international protection lodged in one of the Member States by a third-country national or a stateless person (recast) ('Dublin III Regulation'), OJ 2013 L 180/31.

Council Directive 2000/78/EC of 27 November 2000 establishing a general framework for equal treatment in employment and occupation OJ 2000 L 303/16.

Directive 2003/88 of the European Parliament and of the Council of 4 November 2003 concerning certain aspects of the organization of working time ('Working Time Directive'), OJ 2003 L 299/9.

Directive 2014/104 of the European Parliament and of the Council of 26 November 2014 on certain rules governing actions for damages under national law for infringements of the competition law provisions of the Member States and of the European Union, OJ 2014 L 349/1.

Council Decision of 13 December 2007 relating to the implementation of Article 9C(4) of the Treaty on European Union and Article 205(2) of the Treaty on the Functioning of the European Union between 1 November 2014 and 31 March 2017 on the one hand, and as from 1 April 2017 on the other, OJ 2009 L 314/73.

Decision of the European Central Bank of 14 May 2010 establishing a securities markets programme, OJ 2010 L 124/8.

Council Decision 2011/167 of 10 March 2011 authorizing enhanced cooperation in the area of the creation of unitary patent protection, OJ 2011 L 76/53.

European Council decision of 22 May 2013 concerning the number of members of the European Commission, OJ 2013 L 165/98.

Decision 2015/1523 establishing provisional measures in the area of international protection for the benefit of Italy and of Greece, OJ 2015 L 239/146.

Decision 2015/1601 establishing provisional measures in the area of international protection for the benefit of Italy and Greece, OJ 2015 L 248/80.

Further reading

There are many textbooks on EU law that offer more detailed discussion of the issues covered in this book as well as suggestions for further reading. The following are among the best:

> Catherine Barnard and Steve Peers (eds), *European Union Law* (Oxford, OUP, 2014).
> Damian Chalmers, Gareth Davies, and Giorgio Monti, *European Union Law: Text and Materials* (Cambridge, CUP, 3rd edn, 2014).
> Paul Craig and Gráinne de Búrca, *EU Law: Text, Cases, and Materials* (Oxford, OUP, 6th edn, 2015).
> Trevor Hartley, *The Foundations of European Union Law* (Oxford, OUP, 8th edn, 2014).
> Robert Schütze, *European Union Law* (Cambridge, CUP, 2015).

Useful collections of essays offering general coverage of the field include the following:

> Anthony Arnull and Damian Chalmers (eds), *The Oxford Handbook of European Union Law* (Oxford, OUP, 2015).
> Paul Craig and Gráinne de Búrca (eds), *The Evolution of EU Law* (Oxford, OUP, 2nd edn, 2011).

There are various handy collections of the texts of the Treaties and selected EU legislation. The following are particularly recommended:

> Nigel Foster (ed.), *Blackstone's EU Treaties and Legislation 2016–2017* (Oxford, OUP, 27th edn, 2016).
> Robert Schütze, *EU Treaties and Legislation* (Cambridge, CUP, 2015).

For accessible coverage of the EU from a non-legal perspective, the following are recommended:

Erik Jones, Anand Menon, and Stephen Weatherill, *The Oxford Handbook of the European Union* (Oxford, OUP, 2012).

John Pinder and Simon Usherwood, *The European Union: A Very Short Introduction* (Oxford, OUP, 3rd edn, 2013).

Anthony Teasdale and Timothy Bainbridge, *The Penguin Companion to European Union* (London, Penguin, 4th edn, 2012).

Index

A

accession agreement 75–6
accession treaty 68
acte clair 109
activism (judicial) 14, 97–8
Advocates General 92–3
AFSJ *see* area of freedom, security
    and justice
Amsterdam Treaty (1997) 21
Anderson, David QC 107
annulment actions 102–5
Antonissen (1991) 7
appeals to the Court of Justice 94
Apple 7
acquis communautaire 67
Aranyosi and Căldăraru (2016) 24
area of freedom, security and
    justice (AFSJ) 21–6, 49
Article 2 TEU 66
Article 3(4) TEU 112
Article 6(3) TEU 75
Article 7 TEU 102
Article 12 EEC 78
Article 48(6) TEU 119
Article 50 TEU 69, 72
Article 51(1) of the Charter of
    Fundamental Rights 74
Article 78(3) TFEU 123
Article 119 TFEU 112–13

Article 122(2) TFEU 119
Article 127(1) TFEU 114
Article 136 TFEU 119, 120
Article 235 EEC (flexibility
    clause) 55–6
Article 255 TFEU 96
Article 258 TFEU 99
Article 260 (3) TFEU 101–2
Article 263 TFEU 102
Article 267 TFEU 105, 106, 107,
    108, 121
Article 273 TFEU 120–1
Article 352 56
Ashton, Catherine 35
Assange, Julian 23

B

banking union 122
Becker (1982) 81
Belgium
    margarine packaging 6
    taxation 15
Bingham, Mr Justice 108–9
Bloomberg speech (2013) 27
Bosman (1995) 9–10
Brasserie du Pêcheur and
    Factorame (1996) 86–7
breaches of EU law 85–8, 99–102
Brexit *see* leaving the EU

British Airports Authority 15
Bundesverfassungsgericht (German
    Federal Constitutional
    Court) 60, 89–90, 118, 121

C

Cameron, David 27, 42, 72
'Cassis de Dijon' case (1979) 9, 12
central and eastern Europe
    countries (CEECs) 66, 67
CFSP *see* Common Foreign and
    Security Policy
Charter of Fundamental Rights
    74, 85
CILFIT v Ministry of Health
    (1982) 109–10
citizens' initiative 46
citizenship of the EU 19–20
civil law 97
CJEU *see* Court of Justice of the
    European Union
Cohn-Bendit case (1978) 81–2
Commission 39–46, 99–102, 104
    enhanced cooperation 50–1
Commission v Belgium (1980) 8
Commission v Cresson (2006) 44
Commission v France (2005) 101
Commission v United Kingdom
    (2003) 15
*Commissioners of Customs and
    Excise v Samex ApS*
    (1983) 108–9
Committee of Permanent
    Representatives
    (COREPER) 34
Committee of the Regions 104
Common Foreign and Security
    Policy (CFSP) 19, 35
common law 97
common market 5–9, 17
    competition 16
Common Travel Area 25
Community method 56
competence creep 26–7

competences 28–31
competition in the common
    market 16
competition law 54–5
conferral 28–9, 55
consistent interpretation
    principle 83–4
Constitutional Treaty (2004) 21,
    63–4, 65
Contracting Parties 120–1
convention method 65
Copenhagen criteria 67
Costa v ENEL (1964) 79, 80
Council (of Ministers) 34–9,
    45, 104
    enhanced cooperation 50–1
    OLP 48
    SLP 52
Court of Auditors 104
Court of Justice 91–3, 120–1
    appeals to 94
    criticisms of 97–8
    members 96
    preliminary rulings procedure
        105–11
Court of Justice of the European
    Union (CJEU) 3–4, 7, 8–11,
    13–14, 19–20, 91–8
    members 96–7
    misconduct cases 43–4
    principles of EU law 88
    ruling on directives 81–2
Cresson, Edith 44
customs union 6, 29

D

Dalli v Commission
    (2015) 44
damages, claims against Member
    States 85–8
Dano (2014) 20
De Gaulle, Charles 35–6
decisions 31, 54–5
Defrenne II (1976) 17, 79, 82

Demetriou, Marie QC 107
democratic deficit 59–60
Denmark
  and the eurozone 114
  migration crisis 123
  opting out of the AFSJ 26
  referendum 26, 62–3
direct actions 91, 94
direct effect 81–3, 86, 88
directives 31, 54, 81–5
discrimination cases 17, 82–3, 84–5
Dominguez v CICOA (2012) 85
Douglas-Scott, Sionaidh 86
Dublin III Regulation 123, 124

E

ECB *see* European Central Bank
economic and monetary union
  (EMU) 14, 19, 49, 112
economic policy 116
EFSF *see* European Financial
  Stability Facility
emergency brake procedure
  48–9
EMU *see* economic and monetary
  union
Enchelmaier, Stefan 13
enhanced cooperation 49–52
environmental protection
  measures 18
equal pay principle 17, 79
ESCB *see* European System of
  Central Banks
ESM *see* European Stability
  Mechanism (ESM) Treaty
euro 19, 112–22
Eurojust 24
Europe of Nations and Freedom
  Group 33
European Anti-Fraud Office
  (OLAF) 25
European Arrest Warrant
  (EAW) 23–6

European Central Bank (ECB) 62,
  104, 113–14, 117
European Coal and Steel
  Community (ECSC)
  Treaty 4–5, 19, 21
European Communities Act
  (1972) 72
European Convention on Human
  Rights (ECHR) 75–6
European Council 33–4, 120
  amendment of Treaties 64–5
  banking union 122
European Court of Human Rights
  (ECtHR) 75–6
European Economic Community
  (EEC) Treaty 5–17, 19, 21
European External Action Service
  (EEAS) 35
European Financial Stability
  Facility (EFSF) 119, 121
European Financial
  Stability Mechanism
  (EFSM) 119
European Parliament 32–3, 104
  SLP 52–3
European People's Party 33
European Public Prosecutor's
  Office (EPPO) 24–5
European Stability Mechanism
  (ESM) Treaty 65, 120, 121
European System of Central Banks
  (ESCB) 114, 121
European Union, foundation
  4–5
Europol 24
Eurosystem 114
eurozone crisis 2, 112–22

F

Faccini Dori v Recreb (1994)
  82–3, 86
financial crash of 2008 116
Fiscal Compact 65, 120–1
fiscal policy 116

'Five Presidents' Report' (2015) 122
flexibility clause (Article 235 EEC) 55–6
football 9–10
force majeure 100
Foreign Affairs Council 35
foreign policy provisions 20
Foster (1990) 83
Foto-Frost v Hauptzollamt Lübeck-Ost (1987) 110
France
  accession treaties 68
  and the eurozone crisis 118
  infringement proceedings 101
Francis, Pope 124
Francovich (1991) 85, 86
free movement 6
  free movement of capital 14–16
  free movement of goods 6–7, 8–9, 11, 12, 13–14
  free movement of people 7–11, 13
  justification of obstacles 11–14
  Single European Act (SEA) 18
  social policy 17
  threats to 16
fundamental rights principle 74–5

G

Gauweiler v Deutscher Bundestag (2015) 89, 90
General Court 93–4
  members 96–7
general principles of law 73–4
German Federal Constitutional Court *see* Bundesverfassungsgericht
Germany
  and the eurozone crisis 118
  references for preliminary rulings 107
Google 16
Google Spain v AEPD 3

Greece
  financial crash of 2008 116, 117–18
  migration crisis 124

H

Habermas, Jürgen 118
Heads of State or Government (HoSG) 33–4, 42
High Representative of the Union for Foreign Affairs and Security Policy 35, 40–1
Hillion, Christophe 68, 70
Hollande, François 118
home affairs 20
horizontal agreements 16
horizontal disputes 78
House of Lords EU Committee 25, 26, 58–9, 95
Hungary, migration crisis 124

I

IMF *see* International Monetary Fund
import duty 77
industrial action 11
infringement proceedings 99–102, 120
Inter-Environment Wallonie v Région Wallone (2012) 79–80
interference by the EU 56–9
intergovernmental conference (IGC) 62
internal market 18
international law 61, 79
International Monetary Fund (IMF) 116, 117
Internationale Handelsgesellschaft (1970) 79
internet, right to be forgotten 3
interpretation vs. validity 110
Inuit (2013) 105

Ireland
  'Buy Irish' case (1982) 11
  Common Travel Area 25
  financial crash of 2008 116
  migration crisis 123
  tax benefits to Apple 7
  voting in referendums 63
Italian law 79

J

joining the EU 66–8
Josemans (2010) 13–14
judges
  in the Court of Justice 91–2
  in the General Court 94
judicial approach of the CJEU
  97–8
Juncker, Jean-Claude 42, 44,
  56–7, 58
justice 20
  European Arrest Warrant
   (EAW) 23–6
  see also area of freedom, security
   and justice

K

Kadi 3
Keck and Mithouard (1993) 9
Kerckhaert (2006) 15
Köbler v Austria (2003) 87
Križan (2013) 109
Kücükdeveci (2010) 84

L

Laval (2007) 11
law, general principles 73–4
law-making 45–6, 47–60
  see also legislative acts
lead candidates see
  Spitzenkandidaten
leaving the EU 68–73
legal acts 54–6, 80–1

legal basis 29
legislative acts 48, 53–4
  subsidiarity and
   proportionality 58
  see also law-making
Lisbon Treaty (2007) 20, 21, 35,
  62, 63–4, 68, 90
  provision for leaving the EU 69
Luxembourg 91
  LuxLeaks 42–3, 44
Luxembourg Compromise
  (1966) 36, 80

M

Maastricht Treaty (Treaty on
  European Union (TEU))
  (1992) 19, 21, 62–3
MacCormick, Sir Neil 89–90
Mangold (2005) 3, 17, 74, 84–5, 98
*Marshall v Southampton and
  South-West Hampshire Area
  Health Authority* (1986)
  82–3, 84
May, Theresa 72
Member States 3–5, 104
  breaches of EU law 85–8, 99–102
  enhanced cooperation 49–52
  in the eurozone 114–15
  free movement of capital 14–16
  free movement of goods 6–7,
   8–9, 11, 12, 13–14
  free movement of people 7–11, 13
  leaving the EU 68–73
  migration crisis 123
  newcomers to the EU 66–8
  references for preliminary
   rulings 107–8
  referendums 62–3
  shared competences 30–2
  SLP 52–3
  voting system 35–8
Members of the European
  Parliament (MEPs) 32–3
Merkel, Angela 122–3

Index

migration 23
migration crisis 2, 122–4
Miller v Secretary of State (2017) 72
misconduct cases 43–4
mobile phone network operators 16
Mogherini, Federica 35
monetary policy 116

N

national courts 88–90
national law 77–80, 83–4
    primacy of EU law over 79–80
national parliaments, involvement
        in legislative acts 58–9
Netherlands
    cannabis purchase in Maastricht
        13–14
    import duty 77
Nice Treaty (2001) 21, 63
Nobel Peace Prize 2
non-privileged applicants 105
Norway, accession treaties 68
Nougayrède, Natalie 117

O

opinions 31, 88
Opinions of Advocates General 93
ordinary legislative procedure
    (OLP) 47–9, 64
outright monetary transactions
    (OMTs) 121
overriding interests 13–14

P

Paris attacks (2015) 23, 123–4
passport union 26
Peers, Steve 25
Pescatore, Pierre 107
pillars of the EU 19
Poland
    migration crisis 124
    voting system 37

police, European Arrest Warrant
    (EAW) 23–6
political accountability 59
political institutions of the
    EU 32–46
political parties 33
Portugal, financial crash of
    2008 116
power balance 27
preliminary rulings procedure
    105–11
President of the Commission 40–2
President of the European
    Council 34
primacy of EU law 79–80, 88–9
Pringle v Ireland (2012) 65,
    74–5, 120
privileged applicants 104
procedure préjudicielle d'urgence
    (PPU) 106
Prodi, Romano 45
proportionality principle 13,
    57–9

Q

qualified majority vote (QMV)
    35–6, 48

R

Rasmussen, Hjalte 80, 81
recommendations 31
references for preliminary
    rulings 91
referendums 62–3
refugees 23
regulations 31, 54–5
Regulatory Fitness and
    Performance Programme
    (REFIT) 57
relocation plan 123–4
resignations 44–5
right to be forgotten 3
right to provide services 7–8

right to take collective action 11
Rompuy, Herman van 34

S

Santer Commission 44–5
Sapod Audic (2002) 11
Schengen Agreements 20, 23, 25,
    49, 65
SEA *see* Single European Act
secondary law 28–46
securities markets programme
    (SMP) 119
semi-privileged applicants 104–5
services, right to provide 7–8
simplified procedures 64
Single European Act (SEA) 18–19,
    21, 36, 62
Single Resolution Mechanism
    (SRM) 122
Single Supervisory Mechanism
    (SSM) 122
'Six Pack' 121–2
Slovakia
    migration crisis 123–4
    Slovak Pensions case (2012) 89
    Supreme Court and
        Constitutional Court 109
Snell, Jukka 15–16
social policy 17
social security systems 48
Spain, voting system 37
Spain and Italy v Council
    (2013) 51
special legislative procedure
    (SLP) 52–3
Spitzenkandidaten/lead
    candidates 40, 42
State aid 7
State liability 86–8
Stauder v Ulm (1969) 74
subsidiarity principle 57–9
Sunday trading laws 9
Sweden, and the eurozone 114
Syriza government, Greece 117

T

Tariefcommissie 77–8
Tatham, Allan 66
tax benefits 7
taxation 15
terrorism, European Arrest
    Warrant (EAW) 23
TFEU *see* Treaty on the
    Functioning of the European
    Union
Timmermans, Frans 57
trade unions 11
Treaties 49–50, 52, 61
    amending 62–5
    competition laws 54–5
    interpretation 97
Treaty of Amsterdam (1997) 21
Treaty Establishing a Constitution
    for Europe (Constitutional
    treaty) (2004) 21, 63–4, 65
Treaty on European Union (TEU)
    (Maastricht Treaty) (1992) 19,
    21, 62–3
Treaty of Lisbon *see* Lisbon Treaty
Treaty of Nice *see* Nice Treaty
Treaty on Stability, Coordination,
    and Governance (Fiscal
    Compact) 65, 120–1
Treaty on the Functioning of the
    European Union (TFEU)
    20–2, 24, 29–30
    OLP 47
Tridimas, Takis 13
Tsipras, Alexis 117
Turkey, migration crisis 124
Tusk, Donald 34
'Two Pack' 121–2

U

United Kingdom (UK)
    blocking of Treaty changes 120
    common law system 25
    Common Travel Area 25

Index

United Kingdom (UK) (*cont.*)
EU referendum (2016) 70–3
and the eurozone 114
migration crisis 123
mobile phone network operators 16
opting out of the AFSJ 25–6
taxation of imports 6–7
Working Time Directive 38–9
United Kingdom v Council (1996) 38–9
United Nations Charter 3
United Nations Security Council 3

V

validity vs. interpretation 110
values 2, 12, 59, 66, 73, 88, 91, 102, 107, 125

Van Gend en Loos v Nederlandse Administratie der Belastingen (1963) 61, 77–8, 107
Varoufakis, Yanis 118
vertical agreements 16
vertical disputes 78
Viking (2007) 10–11
voting system 35–8

W

Weatherill, Stephen 82
Weiler, Joseph 59–60
welfare benefits 20
withdrawal *see* leaving the EU
workers, rules on 9–11
Working Time Directive 38–9, 58, 85

European Union Law

SOCIAL MEDIA
Very Short Introduction

Join our community

www.oup.com/vsi

- Join us online at the official Very Short Introductions **Facebook** page.
- Access the thoughts and musings of our authors with our online **blog**.
- Sign up for our monthly **e-newsletter** to receive information on all new titles publishing that month.
- Browse the full range of Very Short Introductions online.
- Read **extracts** from the Introductions for free.
- If you are a teacher or lecturer you can order inspection copies quickly and simply via our website.

ONLINE CATALOGUE
A Very Short Introduction

Our online catalogue is designed to make it easy to find your ideal Very Short Introduction. View the entire collection by subject area, watch author videos, read sample chapters, and download reading guides.

http://global.oup.com/uk/academic/general/vsi_list/

LAW
A Very Short Introduction
Raymond Wacks

Law underlies our society - it protects our rights, imposes
duties on each of us, and establishes a framework for the
conduct of almost every social, political, and economic activity.
The punishment of crime, compensation of the injured, and the
enforcement of contracts are merely some of the tasks of a
modern legal system. It also strives to achieve justice, promote
freedom, and protect our security. This *Very Short Introduction*
provides a clear, jargon-free account of modern legal systems,
explaining how the law works both in the Western tradition and
around the world.

www.oup.com/vsi

THE EUROPEAN UNION
A Very Short Introduction
John Pinder & Simon Usherwood

This *Very Short Introduction* explains the European Union in plain English. Fully updated for 2007 to include controversial and current topics such as the Euro currency, the EU's enlargement, and its role in ongoing world affairs, this accessible guide shows how and why the EU has developed from 1950 to the present. Covering a range of topics from the Union's early history and the ongoing interplay between 'eurosceptics' and federalists, to the single market, agriculture, and the environment, the authors examine the successes and failures of the EU, and explain the choices that lie ahead in the 21st century.